Project Management Institute

Manage to Lead
Flexing Your Leadership Style

Cynthia Stackpole Snyder, PMP, EVP, MBA

Library of Congress Cataloging-in-Publication Data

Stackpole, Cynthia, 1962-
  Manage to lead : flexing your leadership style / Cynthia Snyder Stackpole.
    p. cm.
  ISBN 978-1-935589-59-4 (alk. paper)
  1. Project management. 2. Leadership. I. Title.
  HD69.P75S687 2012
  658.4'092—dc23

                                    2012035396
  ISBN: 978-1-935589-59-4

Published by: Project Management Institute, Inc.
                  14 Campus Boulevard
                  Newtown Square, Pennsylvania 19073-3299 USA
                  Phone: +610-356-4600
                  Fax: +610-356-4647
                  Email: customercare@pmi.org
                  Internet: www.PMI.org

PMI Publications welcomes corrections and comments on its books. Please feel free to send comments on typographical, formatting, or other errors. Simply make a copy of the relevant page of the book, mark the error, and send it to: Book Editor, PMI Publications, 14 Campus Boulevard, Newtown Square, PA 19073-3299 USA.

To inquire about discounts for resale or educational purposes, please contact the PMI Book Service Center.

              PMI Book Service Center
              P.O. Box 932683, Atlanta, GA 31193-2683 USA
              Phone: 1-866-276-4764 (within the U.S. or Canada) or +1-770-280-4129 (globally)
              Fax: +1-770-280-4113
              Email: info@bookorders.pmi.org

10 9 8 7 6 5 4 3 2 1

Table of Contents

Chapter 1

What is Leadership?

Key Points

- Leadership is situational and personal.
- There are certain behaviors exhibited by good project leaders.
- Project leaders demonstrate specific skills.
- There are some common traits and characteristics in leaders.

Topic 1 Leadership is not One-Size-Fits-All

Leadership is a tricky thing to define. It has been defined as the ability to bring like-minded people together to get remarkable things done. Another definition is that leadership is influencing others to support you in the accomplishment of a common task. Regardless of the definition, leadership requires a leader and one or more followers. In the context of project management, we are going to use the project manager in the role of the leader and the project team in the role of the followers.

> **Skill:** an ability acquired through deliberate effort, to carry out complex activities or job functions
>
> **Behavior:** a manner of conducting oneself; a response to an action, environment, person or stimulus
>
> **Knowledge:** being aware; a familiarity gained through experience or association

As difficult as it is to define leadership, it is equally difficult to define the qualities that make a good leader. As far back as Plato, great minds have attempted to determine what makes a great leader. This inquiry focused on the inherent traits in a person that seemed to equate to successful leadership. The "trait" theory of leadership is not as prevalent now. Most leadership models today depict leadership as being situational. For example, there are some situations that call on leaders to be dynamic and visionary, while others call on leaders to be people oriented and develop strong teams. Still other situations rely on a strong intellect and task focus to develop strategies and tactics to deal with complex situations.

For the purposes of this book, we will look at leadership as a competency. A competency is a combination of knowledge, skills and behavior used to improve performance. If a person has leadership competency, they can apply leadership in different situations and contexts. A competent leader will interpret a situation in context and have a repertoire of possible actions. As you develop competence in leadership, you hone your ability to determine the appropriate actions in different situations. In other words, leadership competence improves with experience.

Consistent with the concept of situational leadership, it can also be said that leadership is personal. One size does not fit all. There is no set of behaviors, skills and knowledge that fits all leaders, all followers and all situations. There are no universal leadership characteristics and there is no "recipe for leadership." However, there *are* skills and behaviors that many effective project leaders have. This book will focus on those skills and behaviors, as well as some knowledge that you need to have to be an effective project leader.

In 2011, the Project Management Institute (PMI) surveyed over 700 project managers from 66 different countries to determine the skills and behaviors that are most influential in delivering projects successfully. I will describe those skills and behaviors that project managers have identified as being the most important to them in leading a project.

Because leadership is such a broad topic, I have limited the coverage to those skills and behaviors that were in the top five for co-located teams and virtual teams. Interestingly, many of the *behaviors* were the same for both co-located and virtual teams, but the *skills* for co-located teams and virtual teams were very different.

As mentioned above, competency also requires knowledge. Of course you need knowledge about the specific industry or technology you work in to lead a project successfully. You also need knowledge about how to *manage* a project, such as planning, organizing, and controlling within a framework or a plan. I believe there are also some important areas of knowledge that you need in order to successfully lead a project. Therefore, in addition to providing information on the skills and behaviors necessary to lead projects successfully, I will also describe some of the leadership knowledge you need.

Topic 2: Leadership Behaviors

Information from the leadership survey was broken down into four regions:

- North America (NA)
- Asia/Pacific (AP)
- Europe/Middle East/Africa (EMEA)
- Latin America (LA)

The information presented represents an overall ranking of behaviors from all regions combined. However, where there are significant differences by region, those will be noted in the text. The top five overall leadership behaviors needed to effectively deliver projects, as defined in this survey, are:

1. **Collaboration.** Working together to achieve a goal
2. **Openness.** Transparency and making relevant information available to all stakeholders
3. **Reliability.** The characteristic of keeping your word and having your actions be consistent what you say
4. **Decisiveness.** The willingness to make a decision
5. **Ethics.** The concepts of right and wrong behavior

Some interesting points to note are that collaboration was ranked in the top five for all regions and was ranked number one for all regions except Latin America, where it was ranked third. We will discuss collaboration when we talk about managing your team in chapter 8 and managing conflict effectively in chapter 10.

Openness was also a quality listed in the top five for all regions. We will talk about openness when we discuss being authentic in chapter 3 and communicating in chapter 7.

Reliability was in the top five characteristics for all regions except Latin America. We will touch on reliability when we discuss building trust in the chapter on building your project team.

Decisiveness was in the top five for all regions. Being decisive is an important aspect of decision making which we discuss in chapter 8.

Because ethics vary by industry and geography we will not discuss ethics, except to say that, throughout history, high moral standards and integrity have been considered key traits in effective leaders.

Topic 3: Leadership Skills

Based on the survey, the top five ranked leadership skills are:

1. **Problem solving.** Being able to clearly articulate the problem and work through the issues to achieve a satisfactory solution
2. **Communicating a vision.** Communicating in such a way that the team and other stakeholders want to participate
3. **Team building.** Taking appropriate actions to improve team performance
4. **Decision-making.** Applying an appropriate method to select the best course of action given several possibilities
5. **Coordinating and balancing conflicting stakeholder interests.** Working with multiple stakeholders to achieve an approach and outcome that is acceptable to all

Problem solving was ranked number one for all regions except for Latin America, where it was tied for third. In chapter 8 where we discuss managing your team, we will define a problem-solving process.

Communicating a vision was ranked in the top five for all regions. We will discuss communication in chapter 7.

Team building was ranked either one or two for all regions, except North America where it tied for fourth. We talk about building a project team in chapter 5 and motivating your team members in chapter 6.

Decision making was ranked in the top five for all regions expect North America where it ranked number seven. We will cover decision making in the chapter 8.

Coordinating and balancing conflicting stakeholder interests was ranked as number three in North America, but did not make the top five in any other region. This skill is not covered directly, but the skills needed to effectively coordinate and balance stakeholder interests can be developed by applying the information in the chapter on communication, critical conversations, and managing conflict.

There are several other skills and areas of knowledge that support being able to effectively lead project teams. We will cover these in a chapter on advanced topics which considers power, different modes of thinking, and other subjects.

Topic 4: Leadership Traits and Characteristics

At the beginning of this chapter, I mentioned that the "trait" theory of leadership is not as prevalent as it was in the past. In this context, a trait is defined as a distinguishing quality. However, studies have found that there are certain traits that are prevalent in many leaders. These include:

- Adaptable
- Flexible
- Enthusiastic
- Positive outlook
- Self-aware
- Honest

In addition, there are certain characteristics that many effective leaders share. These include:

- Accountable
- Authentic
- High expectations

- High emotional intelligence
- Clear vision
- Clear communication
- Good decision-maker
- Knows and cares about employees
- Calm in the face of adversity
- Able to inspire and bring out the best in others
- Has self-confidence and self-respect
- Good problem solver

Some of these characteristics and traits were identified when we talked about skills and behaviors needed to effectively manage a project, such as clear communication and good decision-making skills. Others are clearly not skill-based, but are rather personality-based, inherent characteristics found in people. By identifying these traits and characteristics within yourself, you can start to identify where your strengths and weaknesses lie in these areas.

As a leader, you will always be in the spotlight. Your team will look to you to see how to act. If you demonstrate a positive outlook, honesty, and flexibility, you are more likely to see those traits and characteristics reflected back to you from your team members. However, if you talk about those traits, but don't act on them, your team will perceive you as being inauthentic and they will lose their trust and respect for you.

To help you develop self-awareness around your own skills, behaviors, traits and characteristics, we will discuss how to identify your values and other aspects of self-awareness in the next chapter. We will also discuss the importance of authenticity and acting in a manner that is consistent with your values.

In the Workplace

Leading projects and project teams can be challenging. Frequently, you have accountability for the outcomes, but you do not always have the authority you need to select team members, direct how they spend their time, or determine how much time they can give to your project. You can't control team member attitudes or behaviors. However, you can maintain a positive and motivating attitude yourself, even in the face of adversity.

Next time you are in a challenging situation, remember some of the traits and characteristics of effective leaders and adopt them. See how you can become adaptable and flexible in the situation. Try to maintain enthusiasm and a positive outlook regardless of the circumstances. Remember, attitude is infectious. Don't let negativity dampen your enthusiasm or your commitment to the project or to your project team.

Reflection Exercise

Review the following traits and characteristics of effective leaders that were identified in the section on *Leadership Traits and Characteristics*.

Traits	Characteristics
• Adaptable • Flexible • Enthusiastic • Positive outlook • Self-aware • Honest	• Accountable • Authentic • High expectations • High emotional intelligence • Clear vision • Clear communication • Good decision-maker • Knows and cares about employees • Calm in the face of adversity • Able to inspire and bring out the best in others • Has self-confidence and self-respect • Good problem solver

Now think about a time when you saw each of those traits or characteristics demonstrated, whether it was you demonstrating it, or someone else. What was impactful about that situation? What can you learn from that situation to build your leadership abilities?

I have filled out an example from my experience to help you see how to use the tool to help you reflect on how demonstrating leadership traits and characteristics can have a positive outcome.

Trait/Characteristic	Demonstration	Impact	Learning
High expectations	When kicking off a project to update the *PMBOK® Guide* I told the project team this would be a very challenging project, but that their efforts would make a difference for thousands of project managers around the globe	The team members were motivated by the opportunity to contribute to their fellow project managers and embraced the challenge	Being forthright about challenges, and setting a high bar for performance, can be motivating, especially when delivered with enthusiasm and commitment

Chapter 2

Know Thyself

Key Points

- To lead others, you must first know yourself.
- Knowing your personal values is a critical part of knowing yourself.
- By identifying your own strengths and weaknesses, you can develop strategies to leverage your strengths and overcome your weaknesses.
- Self-reflection is the path to self-knowledge.

Topic 1: The Importance of Self-Awareness

When the 75 members of the Advisory Council to the Stanford Graduate School of Business were asked to recommend the most important capability for their leaders to develop, their answer was nearly unanimous: self-awareness.[i]

Self-awareness allows you to exercise self-control, to know when you need to shift into "neutral" instead of getting emotional and blowing up. Knowing yourself and being in control of yourself when you are in a leadership position is absolutely required to maintain credibility and viability as a leader.

You may be thinking, "Now wait a minute, of course I know myself! I have lived with myself for all my life!" Indeed you have, but when I talk about knowing yourself, I am talking about identifying and articulating your values, your strengths and your weaknesses.

> *"All of us have the spark of leadership in us, whether it is in business, in government or as a nonprofit volunteer. The challenge is to understand ourselves well enough to discover where we can use our leadership gifts to serve others."*
>
> —Ann Fudge, former chairman and CEO of Young & Rubicam Brands, and an appointee by President Barack Obama to the National Commission on Fiscal Responsibility and Reform (NCFRR)

---

[i] Bill George, et al. *HBR's 10 Must Reads on Leadership. Discovering Your Authentic Leadership* (Boston: Harvard Business Review Press, 2011).168.

When was the last time you sat down and really thought about your core values? If you are dissatisfied with your work or with someone in your workplace, I bet you can point to a conflict in values as being at the heart of the dissatisfaction. That being said, you need to be able to describe your values in order to identify what is important to you, as well as to identify where conflicting values can cause problems.

Self-knowledge comes with reflecting on your values, your strengths and your weaknesses. In the previous chapter we talked about leadership behaviors, skills, traits, and characteristics. One way to begin to enhance your self-awareness is the *Reflection Exercise* from Chapter 1.

In addition to identifying the leadership traits and characteristics you have, or don't have, you should spend some time really understanding your personal values.

Topic 2: Identifying Your Personal Values

Identifying your values means being able to identify what is important to you. Your values influence how you behave and how you evaluate people and events.

Reflecting on your values helps you to:

- Set standards for yourself and your team;
- Establish principles you can use to make decisions;
- Resolve dilemmas and conflicts; and
- Set a benchmark for your behavior.

To begin to identify your values, start with what is important to you. The following is an incomplete list of words that can help you start to identify what is important in your life. Not all of them are values, but

> In the 2011 PMI survey, "values appreciation" is ranked in the top 10 for both co-located and virtual teams.

you will start to see a pattern or trend in the words that you pick. This should give you an idea about what is most important to you. Take a few minutes to jot down those words that resonate with you.

Work satisfaction	Creativity	Independence
Public service	Aesthetics and beauty	Recognition
Leadership	Management	Excitement and adventure
Social interaction	Self-directed	Financial gain
Competition	Change and variety	Physical challenge
Influencing others	Stability	Mental challenge
Knowledge and mastery	Detailed work	Collaborative work
Recreation and fitness	Security	Individual work
Moral fulfillment	Community	Interacting with others
Self-expression	Communication	

Now add other words to your list that describe what is important to you.

What patterns or trends did you notice?

Did anything surprise you?

Did you notice any areas where your work or home life are inconsistent with your the words you selected?

To identify your core values, distill the list down to approximately five key words that describe what you feel is most important. These are your core values. You should use your core values to help you make decisions, analyze your behavior and guide your actions. You will find that when you are behaving in a way that is consistent with your core values, you are happier and more productive.

There is a *Reflection Exercise* at the end of this chapter that will help you understand how your values shape your behavior.

Topic 3: Defining What Motivates You

Knowing what motivates you is a different aspect of knowing yourself than being able to identify your values. We will spend more time talking about motivation theories in Chapter 6. However, since this chapter is about self-awareness, we will discuss it briefly here.

You can start to identify what motivates you by understanding where you spend your time and energy. Take a few moments to answer these questions either by writing them down or thinking about them.

What situations cause you to want to go above and beyond in your performance?

In which situations would you do things on a volunteer basis because you believe in the cause?

What do you like to do when you're not working?

How would you rank the following "rewards" in relative importance, with 6 being a reward of the highest importance and 1 a reward of the lowest importance?

- Achievement
- Money
- Recognition
- Security
- Independence
- Reputation

Take a look and see if your current environment is consistent with what motivates you. If it is, you are probably pretty satisfied with your job. However, if you are motivated by security and you are in a fairly volatile and uncertain work environment, you may feel stressed out. You may need to work with your organization to design a reward or motivation structure that is aligned with your motivational preferences.

According to Harvard Business Review's (HBR) *Top 10 in Leadership,* most leaders are motivated by achievement rather than external rewards. These people are passionate about their work, seek out challenges, love to learn and take pride in doing their job well.[ii]

Brain Fact

Motivation is fueled by establishing goals and an optimistic outlook. This results in hope for or expectation of a positive outcome, which in turn releases dopamine from the pre-frontal cortex, a "feel-good" chemical. That is why striving for a goal can be so rewarding and feel so good.[1]

Topic 4: Identifying Your Strengths and Weaknesses

We all know there are some things we are good at, and others that we are not so good at. There is value in being able to clearly define and describe our strengths and weaknesses. That way we can play to our strengths in the team environment and staff our team with people who can augment our weaknesses.

Since our performance is better in those areas where we are strong, and we usually enjoy doing those things we are good at, identifying our strengths is a good way to excel in our role. In fact, it is more productive to focus on emphasizing and growing our strengths than it is to overcome our weaknesses. That is not to say that we should not take the time to identify our weaknesses or never worry about them again. Rather, the time you invest in a growing a strength will increase productivity more than the time you spend overcoming a weakness. Therefore, we should develop our talents and understand our weaknesses so that we leverage our strengths and our weaknesses don't undermine our success.

The list below will help you identify your strengths and weaknesses. Look at how each statement below relates to you and score each statement on a scale of 1 to 5 with 1 being low *(this statement is not true about me)* and 5 being high *(this statement describes me well).*

> _____ *I work hard and am productive*
> _____ *I am skilled in turning thoughts in to action*
> _____ *I am flexible and can adapt well to change*
> _____ *I have the ability to identify the cause and effect of choices*
> _____ *I am rational and logical*
> _____ *I am organized and can figure out ways to make complex scenarios work*
> _____ *I can take control of a situation and make decisions*
> _____ *I find it easy to articulate my thoughts and feelings*

[ii]Daniel Goleman. *What Makes a Leader* (Boston: Harvard Business Review, 2004).

_____ *I like to understand the past and draw parallels to the present*

_____ *I think through decisions and choices and contemplate the associated risks and opportunities*

_____ *I enjoy helping others excel*

_____ *I like to work in a structured and routine environment*

_____ *I am empathetic with others*

_____ *I am good at prioritizing my work and following through with actions*

_____ *I am skilled in developing a vision for the future*

_____ *I am comfortable building consensus. I value relationships over results.*

_____ *I like to think about new ideas and opportunities*

_____ *I like to make sure everyone participates in decisions and activities*

_____ *I enjoy learning and collecting information on new concepts*

_____ *I appreciate time to think about situations and enjoy intellectual stimulation*

_____ *I like learning new things and improving my performance*

_____ *I am honest and loyal*

_____ *I am enthusiastic and have an infectious energy*

_____ *I enjoy building and sustaining personal relationships*

_____ *I take ownership for my actions.*

_____ *I have the ability to articulate and solve problems*

_____ *I have confidence in my ability to excel and overcome adversity*

_____ *I am independent and can work without a lot of oversight*

_____ *I can assimilate a lot of information and determine trends and themes*

_____ *I am skilled at building teams and coalitions*

Now that you have scored those statements, identify the top five and the bottom five and enter them into the Strength/Weakness chart below.

My Strengths	My Weaknesses
1. 2. 3. 4. 5.	1. 2. 3. 4. 5.

Use the information from your strength and weakness assessment to optimize your leadership behaviors. For example, if one of your strengths is helping others excel, you will probably adopt a coaching and mentoring leadership style, whereas that might be ineffective if your strength was in taking control of situations and making decisions. On the other hand, if you find yourself needing to be very collaborative and inclusive, and building teams and coalitions is one of your weaknesses, you may need to get some coaching to help you overcome that weakness.

Topic 5: The Importance of Self-Reflection

The work you have done on understanding your values, motivators, strengths and weaknesses will help you become more self-aware. The more self-aware you are, the better you will understand your actions and reactions. You can use that information to be deliberate in how you interact with your team members and stakeholders.

To deepen your self-knowledge, you need to take time out for self-reflection. Taking the time for self-reflection actually accelerates your ability to be a good leader. Self-reflection enables you to notice and see things that may not have been immediately apparent when an experience occurred. You can gain insights into each experience by noticing how you behaved compared to your values, and how you felt about the experience. You can look at your strengths and weaknesses and see the role each played in an experience, and see how you might choose a different behavior in the future if necessary.

You can practice self-reflection by establishing a quiet environment where you can spend some uninterrupted time alone. Then go through the following steps:

1. Notice how you behave in groups, in adverse situations and in public settings.
2. Question yourself about why you behave and think and feel the way you do.
3. Question the assumptions and beliefs that lead you to behave and think the way you do.

Topic 6: Being Authentic

For the final topic in this chapter, we will consider what it means to be authentic. An authentic leader knows themselves and their values, and acts in a manner that is consistent with his or her values. Described another way, self-awareness involves knowing yourself and understanding your values, motivations, strengths and weaknesses. Authenticity means acting from that awareness.

You have probably heard the saying "Do as I say, not as I do." How inspired are you to follow a leader with that attitude? I know I am inclined to run the other way! I don't trust someone who can't do what he or she is asking me to do.

On the other hand, when I see a leader who is the first to tackle the difficult subjects, or pitch in and do the hard work, I am much more inspired to join in and follow their lead.

Part of being an authentic leader is practicing your values consistently. This means that there should be integrity and alignment between what a leader says and what he or she does. They model the behavior they want to see.

Part of being authentic is being open and honest about what motivates you and why you are making particular choices or taking particular actions, even when those actions and decisions aren't popular. You should be able to align those actions and decisions to your values and/or the values of the project team and the organization.

> "No one can be authentic by trying to imitate someone else. . .People trust you when you are genuine and authentic, not a replica of someone else[iii]."
>
> _____
> [iii]ibid. 163.

All of this is not to say that you can't adapt your style to the situation. In fact, it is important to flex your leadership style to meet the needs of the environment, the people and the situation. However, don't flex your values. If you can stay true to your values and your standards of behavior and still achieve your desired outcome, then you are flexing your style effectively.

If you are in a situation where you need to exercise a behavior that you don't consider one of your strengths, then find a way to tailor that behavior to your own unique form of self-expression. For an example of how to flex your style and still remain authentic, consider the following case study.

Case Study

Jenna is a project manager who values openness and inclusiveness. She has identified collaboration and team building as two of her strengths. Jenna has just been put on a project with a very tight deadline and the project scope can't be negotiated. She knows that during the project she is going to have to make decisions that aren't popular. She also knows that there will be times when she will not have the time to work through issues to reach either a collaborative outcome or a compromise.

During the project kick-off meeting, Jenna reviews the project charter and the competing demands for the project with the team. She suggests that the team develop a team charter that includes a process for decision-making, one for those that are not time-critical and one for those that are. Given the time-sensitive nature of the project, Jenna suggests that for time-critical decisions she will consult with the team, with an understanding that she will make a decision if the team cannot reach consensus in a timely manner. The team agrees that this is an acceptable approach and documents it in the team charter (for more information on a team charter, see Chapter 5).

This outcome is consistent with Jenna's values of openness because she is communicating to her team the potential for situations that might cause her to operate in a way that is not consistent with her appreciation for and strength in collaboration. In essence, she has flexed her style to include a more autocratic method of leadership while remaining authentic and aligned with her values.

Tools You Can Use

There are many tools on the web that you can access to identify your values, your strengths and your weaknesses. Most of them are designed around career coaching or general management, so you will have to tailor them to the project scenario. A few of the web sites I found that were particularly helpful include:

- www.rileyguide.com
- www.mindtools.com
- www.humanmetrics.com

Reflection Exercise

Our values shape our behaviors in ways we aren't always aware of. You can develop a deeper level of self-awareness by identifying the meaning behind your values and describing how that value has shaped your behavior. I have filled out one row so you can see how it works.

Value	Meaning	Shape
Honesty	Don't lie. Don't hide the truth. Don't mislead.	I will go out of my way to make sure people understand my meaning and intention. I confront possible areas of *misunderstanding* up front. I say what I mean and don't necessarily go with the crowd.

Reflection Exercise

You are a self-aware leader if these statements are true of you:

1. I know my strengths and weaknesses.
2. I understand my goals, dreams, and hopes.
3. My work and my values match.
4. I take time to reflect.

Chapter 3

Emotional Intelligence

Key Points

- Emotional intelligence is a defining factor in the difference between a leader by position and a great leader.
- Self-awareness is the first component of emotional intelligence.
- The ability to manage your emotions and behaviors is part of self-management.
- Empathy and the ability to understand non-verbal cues from others are important aspects of social awareness.
- Social skills are what emotionally intelligent leaders use to lead groups of people effectively.

Topic 1: What is Emotional Intelligence?

You may have heard the term "emotional intelligence" over the years, and you may even have some idea of what it means. For this chapter, we are going to delve into emotional intelligence and how it plays a role in effective leadership.

In the 1990s, two researchers from Yale, Salovey and Mayer, started using the term "emotional intelligence, "then defined as "the ability to perceive emotion, integrate emotion to facilitate thought, understand emotions, and regulate emotions to promote personal growth." Using this definition, they considered emotional intelligence a type of intelligence based on a person's abilities. In 1995, Daniel Goleman published *Emotional Intelligence*, a popular book that launched an interest in emotional intelligence which continues today. There is some disagreement about whether there really is such a thing as "emotional intelligence" which can be tested or disproved. Some of these debates include whether emotional intelligence can be proven to be different than cognitive intelligence or whether emotional intelligence is a collection of traits that can be identified.

There are also varying definitions of emotional intelligence and some differing opinions on the components that make up emotional intelligence. For the purposes of our discussion, the following definition and model will be used to discuss emotional intelligence:

Definition

Awareness of one's own emotions and moods and those of others, especially in managing people[i]

[i]*Collins English Dictionary* - Complete & Unabridged 10th Edition (*Needs place of publication*: William Collins Sons & Co Ltd, 2009).

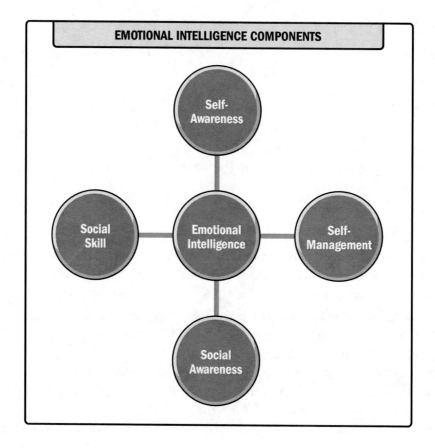

When we talk about intelligence we tend to think about IQ and cognitive abilities. We generally think that those who are successful in high-level jobs have a higher IQ and well-developed technical skills in their field. But we don't often think about the ability of high-level managers to identify and manage their emotions, or their ability to perceive and work with the emotions of their employees.

However, research has shown that IQ and technical skills are threshold capabilities for successful executives. That means that you can't get to that level without being reasonably intelligent and having excellent technical skills in your field.

The discriminating factor in what makes someone successful at the higher levels of management, however, is their emotional intelligence, not their cognitive abilities or their technical skills. It is their self-awareness and management, and their social awareness and skills. Emotional intelligence sets apart which executives, professionals, or scientists will be the best leaders.[ii]

> Your ability to have good relationships with others gets you farther in business and in your personal life than your IQ. It's not how smart you are that counts, but rather how you are smart.[1]

Emotional intelligence is the critical distinction between great leaders and people that have risen in the hierarchy based on their position. According to Daniel Goleman, a person can have the best training in the world, an incisive, analytical mind, and an endless supply of smart ideas, but he still won't make a great leader.[iii]

> In the Johnson and Johnson Company they did a study and found that in divisions around the world, those identified at mid-career as having high leadership potential were far stronger in EI competencies than were their less-promising peers.

In fact, the higher a person rises in an organization, the more important emotional intelligence becomes. In senior leadership positions, nearly 90% of the difference in successful leaders is attributable to emotional intelligence factors rather than cognitive ones.[iv]

Topic 2: A Little More on Self-Awareness

The first component of EI is self-awareness. Though we covered self-awareness in the previous chapter, since it is the first component of emotional intelligence I want to say a few more words about it in the context of EI.

The aspects of self-awareness that are most prevalent when discussing emotional intelligence are recognizing and understanding your moods and emotions and how they impact you, your job performance and your team members. For

- Recognize your moods and emotions
- Conduct realistic self-assessment
- Possess Self-confidence

example, if you know you get really stressed when you are up against a tight time deadline, you should endeavor to get your work done early rather than wait until the last minute.

[ii]Daniel Goleman *Daniel Goleman on Leadership and the Power of Emotional Intelligence (Forbes, 2011)*.
[iii]Daniel Goleman. *What Makes a Leader* (Boston: Harvard Business Review, 2004).
[iv]HBR. ibid.

Another aspect of self-awareness is the ability to assess yourself realistically. We talked about knowing your strengths and weaknesses in the last chapter. Knowing your strengths and weaknesses allows you to have confidence and know how you can best contribute to your team, your project and your organization. If you know yourself to be a skilled facilitator, you can feel confident in stepping up to facilitate a meeting, or coaching a team member in developing her facilitation skills. Conversely, if you are aware that you tend to be uncomfortable in a conflict environment and that you tend to give in too easily, you can point out that you may not be the best person to negotiate a contract with a vendor.

One of the benefits of self-awareness is that once you have defined your values, you often make career decisions that mesh with your values, and consequently, you will tend to enjoy work more and excel in your position.

Topic 3: Self-Management

Self-management, or self-regulation, as it is sometimes referred to, is the ability to think before acting. It entails suspending snap judgments and impulsive decisions and choices. This allows us to redirect the less productive choices we may feel tempted to make. Let's look at a scenario.

Scott is the project manager for a very technical project. His team is predominately comprised of engineers, scientists and technical staff. Scott has an undergraduate degree in engineering, but not the advanced degree that most of the

- Trustworthiness
- Ability to handle change
- Comfort with uncertainty
- Integrity

people on his team have. However, he is very level-headed and thinks before he acts. The team is meeting to help problem-solve some performance issues for one of the components that isn't working as it should.

Scott opens the meeting by outlining the target performance and identifying the gap in performance they are currently experiencing. Sterling, one of the senior technicians, who is clearly agitated, interrupts and states, "What would you know about problem-solving the issue we're having? You can't even begin to understand the technical details involved!"

That kind of condescending remark could definitely result in a team leader wanting to respond with an equally insulting comment, such as "If you could get your head out of a technical manual long enough to properly frame the issue, you might have a chance at figuring out how to resolve it. But it seems that you are more interested in whining and complaining than actually fixing the situation!"

Fortunately, in this scenario, Scott exercises self-management and keeps from blowing up. He steps back and assesses the situation, reflecting on how the technical team is likely very frustrated with the situation. He uses this information to help determine an appropriate path forward by allowing the team some time to vocalize their frustration before outlining a problem-solving approach that he thinks will help frame the problem and outline criteria for possible solutions before a brainstorming session.

This self-managing behavior actually builds trust and credibility with the team. The team now trusts that Scott is not going to have an impulsive reaction to a difficult encounter. It also models the type of behavior Scott wants to see on the team. This example shows that good leaders start by leading themselves.

People who are self-managing are also able to handle change and ambiguity better. We all know that change and ambiguity are an almost constant state of affairs on projects. This makes leaders more flexible and adaptable to the environment.

A person who is skilled in self-management is more likely to make decisions based on their values. It takes self-awareness to identify your values, but it takes self-management to act consistently with those values, especially in stressful situations. It is this behavior of acting consistently with your values, especially in difficult situations, that establishes integrity or authenticity. Integrity, in this scenario, means acting consistently and in alignment with your values.

The part of the brain that corresponds to self-management is the amygdala. The amygdala is part of the limbic system and, among other functions, processes emotional reactions. The amygdala is the component of the brain that governs the fight, flight, and freeze reactions. When a person is highly stressed, the amygdala can take over the higher functioning parts of the brain and, in effect, hijack the brain. This was important when our ancestors had to make an immediate decision on whether to flee or fight or freeze. Fortunately, in the business world we are rarely in a flight, flight, or freeze situation. Unfortunately, the amygdala still sometimes takes over as if we were. In his e-book *The Brain and Emotional Intelligence: New Insights*, Daniel Goleman identifies the top five triggers in the workplace as:

1. Condescension and lack of respect
2. Being treated unfairly
3. Lack of appreciation
4. Believing you are not being listened to
5. Being held to unrealistic deadlines[v]

As project managers we have all been in situations where we have faced being held to unrealistic deadlines. The ability to rationally explain why the expectations are unrealistic in a calm manner demonstrates self-management, especially when coupled with the concern that you aren't being listened to and are being set up to fail!

---

[v]Daniel Goleman. *The Brain and Emotional Intelligence: New Insights* (North Hampton, MA: More Than Sound LLC, *year?*).

Topic 4: Social Awareness

Social awareness is a state of being aware of the emotional condition of others. This is also referred to as empathy. Social awareness is critical in a project environment, whether that team is virtual or co-located. Emotionally intelligent leaders consider their team members' feelings - along with other factors such as impending deadlines, project risks, and customer expectations - when making decisions.

Considering a single team member's feelings is not so difficult, but things get much more challenging when you have a team of eight or ten people. Everyone has their own points of view and there may be

- Aware of how others feel
- Ability to read non-verbal cues
- Empathy

alliances and hidden agendas. Your role is to make sense of and understand what is going on with everyone so you can effectively lead the team to consensus. No wonder leading a team can seem so challenging sometimes!

Your team members probably have more demands on their time than they know how to meet. How they feel around you plays a large role in their level of motivation and commitment to your project. I am sure you can remember a time when you *wanted* to work harder to deliver for someone you respected or someone who made you feel good about yourself. That is what social awareness and empathy is about.

Social awareness or empathy has three parts:

- Cognitive awareness is the ability to understand how another person sees events and the world. For example, a person who comes from a military background is more prone to want to understand the 'mission' or objective of the project, report on the facts and respect position authority. Someone with a background in social services might be focused on how people feel and whether everyone is being included in a conversation. Both viewpoints are valid, but they are different. The socially aware project leader recognizes the difference in how they see the environment.

- Emotional awareness is an ability to understand how another person feels. The above-mentioned military person might not have many feelings attached to receiving constructive feedback on a deliverable, even if it is given in a perfunctory and clipped tone of voice. The same style of feedback given to a more 'sensitive' person could cause them to feel rejected or hurt or not good enough. For such a person,

The six universal feelings are:

- Happiness
- Sadness
- Anger
- Frustration
- Disgust
- Fear

This means that around the world these are the 6 emotions that are consistent and show up in facial expressions.[1]

the socially skilled project manager may want to provide that feedback in a softer tone of voice with some explanation of why the feedback is necessary and how other aspects of their performance is really great.

- Empathic concern or sympathy is another aspect of social awareness. This can include reflecting back the emotion someone is feeling and putting one-self in their shoes to understand what they are going through.

Social awareness is what allows you to understand what is going on behind the words. It includes tuning into a person's tone of voice, gestures, facial expressions, and body language. Consider the following case study.

Case Study

Robin is leading a weekly team meeting with her project management team. The participants in this meeting include Ella, Lou, Michael (Lou's boss), and John. Robin opens the meeting by reviewing the agenda, which includes an update from Lou on a deliverable that is due this week and a report from John on a brainstorming session he had with a some of the other project team members (not on this management team).

Robin starts by asking Lou to update the team on his deliverable. As Lou starts speaking, Robin notices that Ella is glancing at her phone quite a bit and fidgeting with her cuticles. When Ella sees Robin notice this, she glances down and away. In the meantime, Lou is mumbling something about being 90% complete, but just needing to resolve a small connector issue. He is looking at his papers. When he says this Michael looks up sharply with his eyes slightly wide and his eyebrows shoot up. His lips get thinner as he stares at Lou. When it is John's turn to talk Robin notices his head is held up and his jaw is jutting out. His voice seems a little louder than normal.

What do you think is happening with each of the team members? How do you think Robin should handle the situation? A leader who is not socially aware might not pick up on these non-verbal cues, or might choose to ignore them, hoping they will go away, or assuming they are not her problem. However, in this case, Robin is socially aware. She takes a moment and asks the team to take a time out from the agenda to talk about what is going on.

First, she asks Ella why she is so distracted. Ella blushes and apologizes. She replies, "I have a big presentation after this meeting, and I am a little nervous about it. I'm sorry for being distracted. I will try to pay more attention."

Next Robin talks to Lou and says, "Lou, I take it Michael thought you were done with the deliverable and was not aware you were having difficulties. Is that correct?" Michael pipes up and says, "You're darn right I wasn't. I shouldn't have to find out in a team meeting!" Robin wisely decides that this issue should be dealt with offline and asks Lou to update her as soon as the issue with the connector is resolved. She sends him a sympathetic look as well.

Finally she asks John how he felt his meeting went. He replies that of course it went fine. He knew the solution all along and convinced his team of it without too much trouble. Robin asks which method of brainstorming or voting the team used to land on a solution. John states that he didn't really use brainstorming or voting. He just laid out the solution as he saw it. Since no one presented what might have been, in his opinion, a better solution, he just implemented his solution. Robin realizes that John has a lot of pride associated with his technical skills and really believes he knows best. However, he is not being a team player and probably forced his opinion on the rest of the team. She makes a note to check in with the other team members and to talk with John about being more collaborative in the future.

The above scenario describes many different emotions. This is not all that uncommon. It is more uncommon for a leader to be aware of what is happening and understand effective ways to lead the team despite those emotional reactions. Social awareness can help you to be an effective leader, but it isn't always easy. The good news is with some practice you can learn to recognize the non-verbal cues and respond appropriately.

> **Brain Fact**
>
> As with self-management, there is a direct correlation to brain activity when someone feels that you understand them. Their brain releases dopamine, serotonin, and endorphins. These are all "feel-good" chemicals. Therefore, having social awareness causes people to want to work with you, because they feel good when they do!

Topic 4: Social Skill

Social skill is the culmination of the other dimensions of emotional intelligence. Social skill is about managing groups of people, such as project teams, building social networks, finding common ground with various stakeholders, and building rapport. The more effective you can be at understanding and managing yourself, the more effective you will be in empathizing with others and thus building relationships, rapport and loyalty.

An important aspect of social skills is the ability to build rapport. In this context, rapport means building a harmonious and sympathetic connection with others. Leadership depends on relationship-building. A socially skilled person will have a

- Effective in building teams
- Able to manage groups
- Builds rapport and relationships

knack for finding common ground with people of all kinds, and building relationships with them. Socially skilled people are good at leading teams and they generally have a wide variety of friends and acquaintances at work and in their personal lives.

Leaders of any kind, including project leaders, need to manage relationships effectively. A project leader can only lead through her ability to build relationships between team members, functional managers, sponsors, customers, and other stakeholders. After all, the project leader's job is to get work done through other people, and social skill makes that possible. Social skill allows project leaders to put their emotional intelligence to work.[vi]

Topic 5: Utilizing Emotional Intelligence

> **Brain Fact**
>
> The size of the amygdala correlates positively with both the size and the complexity of social networks. Individuals with larger amygdalae have larger and more complex social networks and were better able to make accurate social judgments about other persons' faces. This finding leads us to assume that larger amygdalae allow for greater emotional intelligence, enabling greater societal integration and cooperation with others.

Another way of looking at emotional intelligence is through intrapersonal and interpersonal intelligence. Intrapersonal intelligence is about your relationship with yourself and interpersonal intelligence is about your relationship with others.

Intrapersonal intelligence

A person with intrapersonal intelligence has the traits of self-awareness and self regulation. They understand their own strengths and weaknesses and reflect on how to optimize their strengths and overcome their weaknesses. These people are self-motivating and use feedback to improve themselves and their performance. They work well alone and are comfortable working on virtual teams.

> **Brain Fact**
>
> People with intrapersonal intelligence use the frontal lobe to integrate feelings from the limbic system and sensory information from the parietal lobe to direct their actions.

Interpersonal intelligence

A person with interpersonal intelligence has the traits of social awareness and social skills. They are very skilled at working with others because of their ability to communicate, recognize moods, intentions and motivations, and build rapport. People feel good around those with interpersonal

> **Brain Fact**
>
> The frontal lobe, right temporal lobe and limbic system work together to understand how others feel and how it relates to the current situation.

[vi]HBR. ibid.

intelligence because they genuinely care about other people. They share themselves openly, including personal stories.

People with interpersonal intelligence make good team leaders because of their ability to work collaboratively with people of all types and their social skills. They are good mediators and facilitators and can effectively resolve conflict.

Topic 6: Increasing Emotional Intelligence

You are an emotionally intelligent leader if these statements are true of you:

1. I recognize my emotions.
2. I am in touch with my body and its responses.
3. I am aware of other's emotions, body language, and tonality.
4. I build rapport with people and can lead teams in productive behavior.
5. I trust my instincts and usually make good decisions.

If you are not comfortable answering yes to all of the above statements, don't worry. You can increase and improve your emotional intelligence. You have probably noticed the "Brain Facts" boxes scattered throughout this chapter. Based on reading those, you may remember that emotional intelligence is largely based in the brain's limbic system, which governs feelings, impulses, and drives. Research indicates that the limbic system learns best through motivation, extended practice, and feedback. This is different from how we learn analytical and technical information. Analytical and technical information is learned through the neocortex, which grasps concepts and logic.

To enhance emotional intelligence, you need to focus on working on the limbic system to break old behavioral habits and establish new ones. For example, if you are in a situation where your emotions take over your behavior in a way that you are not happy with, take some time to reflect on what was going on inside your head. See if you can remember what your inner dialogue was saying that impacted your feelings and mood. If you can recognize the influences that caused you to behave a certain way, you can manage them better in the future. Try these steps next time you are situation that requires you to manage your emotions:

1. Identify the people, situations, or events that triggered your emotional reaction.
2. Reflect on the triggers and learn to recognize them.
3. Determine appropriate responses for each trigger.
4. Talk to yourself about how you will react to a similar situation in the future. You can even visualize the event happening with a new outcome.

Make sure to go easy on yourself. Learning new behaviors takes time. You are creating new habits. Make sure to congratulate yourself when you behave more productively in the future. A little positive self-talk always helps! Remember to have empathy for yourself as well as others. The good news is that emotional intelligence tends to increase with age. Sometimes we call this maturity, sometimes the school of hard knocks, but we do learn.

In the Workplace

To increase your ability to tune in to people's emotions and feel empathy, try these techniques:

1. Focus on their body language, gestures, and tone of voice.
2. If you see someone who is saying one thing, but their body language and tone are saying another, take a moment and check in with them.
3. Ask them how they are doing or if there is anything going on that is distracting them or bothering them.

To improve your social skills, when you talk to someone, follow these guidelines:

1. Give them your full attention without distractions.
2. Ignore your phone, messages, texts, and other distractions, and focus on the person you are with.
3. Make eye contact.
4. Pay attention to your non-verbal cues and make sure you maintain an open and attentive posture.

Increase your social awareness in meetings with the following:

1. Pay attention to the person speaking.
2. Don't bring, or don't answer, your phone, email or texts.
3. Be mindful of yourself. If you are distracted, put those thoughts aside and be present to what is happening in the moment.

Tools You Can Use

There are many tools on the web that assess emotional intelligence. A few of the web sites I found that were particularly helpful include:

- http://greatergood.berkely.edu/ei_usquiz
- http://personality-testing.info/tests/EI.php
- www.queendom.com/tests/

Chapter 4

Leadership Styles

Key Points

- We each have a preference for thinking strategically or tactically.
- Our personality influences how we lead.
- There are different leadership roles that we can fulfill in leading a project.

There is no shortage of leadership models that define "leadership styles." You might see a list of leadership styles, such as:

- Democratic
- Facilitative
- Autocratic
- Transformational

Each of these "styles" has a description of the behaviors associated with the style. This is useful information when you want to identify either models of behavior or stereotypes. However, none of us has one fixed style that is appropriate for every situation. We need to be able to flex our leadership style based on numerous factors, such as:

- Personal strengths
- Personality
- Type of leadership role
- Team member experience and expertise
- Organizational environment
- Urgency of the situation
- Importance of the long-term relationship

Since we can't do much about the bottom four bullets, I want to focus on how our thinking style, personality and the type of leadership role we are playing combine to meet the needs of the situation. For thinking style, we will compare strategic thinking and tactical planning. Next we'll look at how our personality influences the way we communicate and demonstrate our leadership strengths. The last aspect of leadership styles we will visit is the "role" required of the leader. By looking at thinking style along with personality, and the defined role of the leader you can determine how to combine and integrate each component to flex your style as is called for by the situation.

Topic 1: Thinking Style

Most people have a dominant strength in either "big-picture" thinking or logistical planning. This is not to insinuate that as leaders we don't need both abilities. We absolutely do. However, each of us tends to lean toward one of these as a key strength more than the other. You may have even listed one of these when you were identifying your strengths in Chapter 2. Strategic thinkers are more of the big-picture thinkers, whereas tactical planners are skilled at determining a path to reach the stated objectives. Let's look at how these strengths are applied to projects.

Strategist

If you are a strategist, you often challenge the status quo or the underlying assumptions that others cling to. You like to focus on the future and how to transform your existing organization. You are good at looking at the external environment, spotting trends, and understanding how a change in the environment and circumstances can interact to bring about an opportunity in the market. You find ways to integrate external factors and your organization's strategy to create an inspiring vision.

As a strategist, you are able to create a vision of what is possible in the future and communicate it across various thinking styles to engage others in your vision. You are probably very comfortable discussing new possibilities with people at all levels, of the organization from the boardroom to the lunchroom, because you are passionate about what you see as possible. Your leadership is focused more on your ability to influence at all levels rather than your authority or position in the organization.

Because many people are resistant to change (not you!), you are comfortable working with conflict. You have a unique way of blending idealism and opportunity with pragmatic realism.

Often, your enthusiasm about the future is contagious and others are motivated and become engaged in your vision because of your excitement and passion. This works well because you tend to be very collaborative and open about sharing the future as you see it.

In the world of project management, a strategist does well with groundbreaking programs, mergers and business transformation projects. They are not so good at day-to-day project management, because the structure and detailed planning is difficult for them to embrace.

Case Study

CustomRev is a company that specializes in building and customizing industrial engines. Winston is a project manager at a CustomRev with a strategic thinking style. Because of Winston's skill in strategic thinking, the Chief Operating Officer approached Winston and said, "Winston, we are currently using seventeen different systems to manage our supply chain. Our order turnaround time is sixty-five days. We currently have a 96 percent order accuracy rate. We need a way to reduce the number of systems, decrease our order fulfillment time, improve our order accuracy and reduce our inventory levels. I want you to head up a project that will accomplish these objectives."

This is a really great project for Winston. It is exactly the type of project at which a strategic project manager can excel. To develop a vision for the project, Winston starts by putting together a team of the internal staff and managers across all the affected departments. The team includes representation from the account management, ordering, inventory, production, quality, shipping, and billing departments.

After several weeks of meetings, brainstorming sessions, and development meetings Winston's team has a good idea of the needs of the various departments. Winston uses that information when he looks outside the organization to identify trends in the supply chain management industry. He looks at trends in his own business and other related businesses. He also consults with the senior executives about their strategic plan for the organization in the next 3 to 5 years.

Using a systems thinking perspective, Winston leads his team in thinking about the entire supply chain operation from end to end to see how to optimize the process. They look for unintended consequences of various designs and search for unidentified opportunities and synergies that they can take advantage of when implementing the new system.

Four months after the COO approached Winston, he presents the team's vision for the new supply chain to the executive committee. Winston is excited about the implications of the project on the business and paints a compelling vision of the future and how this project can transform the way the organization does business.

The Planner

If you are a planner, project management is probably a very comfortable home for you. You like to focus on objectives, deliverables, and milestones and how to accomplish them. You are driven by achievement. You may use your analytic abilities to figure out the best way to approach a project, or you may enjoy working with a team to determine how to accomplish the project objectives.

A leader who is strong in planning can create a supportive atmosphere for their team to carry out the work. They provide a structured approach to make sure the team wins and reaches the project goals. This type of leader is very skilled in balancing the competing demands of the project. They can make tradeoffs between scope, schedule, resources, risk, cost, and quality, and understand the impacts and implications of their choices.

Team members who work with this type of leader generally appreciate the clear and unambiguous targets and the straight-forward method of setting a goal, planning how to get there and carrying out that plan. The planner is skilled at removing road-blocks and uses reason and logic to achieve their desired outcomes. They are not afraid to roll up their sleeves and do the work if needed.

The planner is a good project manager when the scope of the project is well-defined and well-understood. Generally, projects that are completed within nine to twenty-four months are a good size for planners. They are not as skilled at dealing with uncertainty as strategists. They like processes that have been proven to work because efficiency helps them achieve their goals.

Case Study

Mason is a project manager at a nuclear generating facility. Periodically, the reactors are taken offline for maintenance. The maintenance process is very tightly controlled, because for every hour that the system is down, the plant loses millions of dollars in electricity generation. Mason has been the project manager for these projects for the last several years because of his detailed planning abilities and his focus on getting the reactor down, serviced and back up again in as short a time as possible while meeting all regulatory and quality requirements.

Mason works with his team to create a detailed schedule, identify and respond to risks, and integrate learning from previous projects into the current project. Prior to the shutdown, the team does a "dry run" so everyone knows what they are supposed to be doing, the order and sequence of the activities, and the measurements metrics required for each step to be completed according to plan. The learning from the "dry run" is integrated into the final plan before being approved by the Plant Manager and the Senior Engineer.

Mason's team, senior management and the safety committee are all comfortable with Mason's logical and steady approach, which they all know is necessary to conduct a successful maintenance shutdown.

Of course we aren't solely strategists or solely planners. These are descriptions of characteristics that feel more natural to us. Think of them as a continuum with the description of a strategist at one end and the description of a planner on the other. We all fall somewhere on that continuum. Depending on the type of project you are working on you may need to flex your style a bit to embrace one end of the spectrum more than the other.

Personality

The next variable that influences our leadership style is our personality. Each of us brings our own personality to our teams. Our personality shapes how we communicate and how we interact with our team and other stakeholders. Some people are very energetic while others are more supportive in nature. In the previous chapter on Emotional Intelligence we talked about self-awareness. Understanding our natural way of being can help us to capitalize on our personality, or inform us of when we need to flex our natural style based on the needs of the situation.

The four personality types are just models. They aren't hard and fast descriptions of personalities. They merely describe patterns of behavior to help us understand our actions so we can select the most effective conduct in a given situation.

Collaborator

Collaborators are relationship based-leaders. They are democratic, inclusive and transparent. They engage their team in meaningful conversations and include them in decisions and problem solving. They strive to use a facilitative style to build consensus and buy in from all stakeholders. This approach can be time consuming, but the result is motivated, productive teams with a high degree of loyalty.

> **In the trenches**
>
> The PMI survey of effective project behaviors showed that collaboration was the most important behavior in managing a project across every geographic region.

A collaborator keeps his or her eye on the project objectives, but considers their team the best way to reach those objectives. This personality type can build a long-term trusting environment. They are good at projects where high morale and trust are important. They are not the best choice for a short-term urgent project.

> **Brain Fact**
>
> When you are in a collaborative environment you feel safe and your brain releases chemicals that make you feel good, this allows your brain to focus at a higher level.

> **Case Study**
>
> Beth is an implementation project manager at a software company. Her firm sells customizable software to the film industry. Her job requires her to manage the implementation of high end software and coordinate her team's work with the customer's implementation team.
>
> Beth excels at her job because she is very customer-focused and takes the time to get to know the customer's implementation team. In her projects she consistently builds trust between her team and the customer team. The two teams end up working very well together to determine the best approach to implementing the software. When there are problems on the project, Beth leads brainstorming and problem solving sessions where all team members participate.
>
> While Beth's projects aren't done as quickly as some of the other project managers in her organization, she has the highest customer satisfaction rating with her implementations.

Energizer

An energizer personality is confident and passionate about what they believe in. Because of this confidence and passion, they can be very persuasive and influential. Energizers are upbeat and have a positive attitude. They are very charismatic people who rally their team to produce results. Energizers usually have a high emotional intelligence. They know themselves and they know how to read other people and influence groups.

Energizers are good project leaders when a project needs short bursts of focused energy and high motivation. However, sometimes team members believe more in the leader than they do in the project. If the leader leaves, or their interest withers, the team may follow.

Case Study

A training company has just gotten an opportunity to bid on a very large training contract. The bid has a short turnaround time and will require the proposal response team to work long hours for the next three weeks. The Sales and Marketing Director has asked Heidi to head up the proposal team because of her excellent reputation for inspiring her teams to deliver high quality work under tight time constraints.

Heidi takes on the project with a high level of enthusiasm. She leads a kickoff meeting with the team describing the great opportunity that winning this proposal would be for the company. She outlines the benefits of the winning the business and also talks about the level of commitment and hard work it is going to take over the next three weeks to deliver a winning proposal.

At the end of the kickoff meeting, the team understands they have a lot of hard work ahead of them, but they are excited about working together and are fully engaged in doing their best work to create a great proposal.

Advocate

An advocate is a supportive but "hands-off" leader. They empower their team to make decisions and they delegate authority as much as possible. There is very little day-to-day oversight. This type of leadership is motivating for teams with higher education and substantial experience that don't need a lot of oversight and supervision.

The advocate encourages and supports the team while allowing them to determine how best to meet the project objectives. This personality type does a good job of promoting the project outside the team, such as to senior management, external stakeholders, and the public.

Team members that are new or inexperienced will be uncomfortable with this type of leadership and may need more direction to succeed.

Jake is a senior project manager who has been in his role at an engineering company for 15 years. He has worked with everyone in the organization and respects their intelligence and dedication to their job. When he manages a project, he develops a statement of work, a high-level milestone schedule, and a budget. During the kickoff meeting, he delegates the detailed development to his team members, letting them know when he needs their detailed plans back.

During the project, Jake leads the team meetings by facilitating any issue resolution or risk discussions that are necessary. As long as all the work is progressing as planned, he takes a very hands-off approach to the project. When a risk event or issue occurs he will work with the team to frame the questions and issues for resolution, but he allows the team to do most of the problem solving on their own.

Much of Jake's role is managing the customer, insuring that the team has the resources they need and making sure the scope is controlled.

This approach works well with the engineers Jake works with because they don't feel he is overly controlling and they feel he respects them to work out any issues on their own.

Director

A director has an authoritarian personality. They know what they want, they set clear expectations, and they expect results. A director does not seek feedback or input from the team members. They step in, take control and expect compliance.

People often consider this type of person to be bossy. The focus is on the task at hand and not on the team or stakeholders. This form of leadership is not generally effective in the long term. However, in emergency situations, when the deliverables are critical or when you have a team you don't know, you may adopt some of the behaviors of this personality until experience shows that you can loosen the reins a bit and adopt a less intense style.

Case Study

Keith is a very fact-driven person. He can be a little abrupt sometimes. Keith also has a very crisp thinking style and he communicates his expectations very clearly. It's not that he is rude; it's just that he knows he can make his best contribution to the company by keeping a tight rein on the scope, schedule and cost of a project.

Keith is frequently called in to rescue projects that have gone off course because he has a clear picture of what needs to happen to fix the situation and he isn't afraid to step on a few toes to get things done.

Survey of Personality Types

The graphic below shows the relative concern for people or tasks, based on the personality type. Leaders with a high task orientation are driven by reaching project objectives. They work with team members to identify a strategy to meet objectives, and they measure and monitor progress towards those objectives.

Leaders with a high people orientation are interested in getting to know the team members and their values. They want the team to work together to achieve the outcomes.

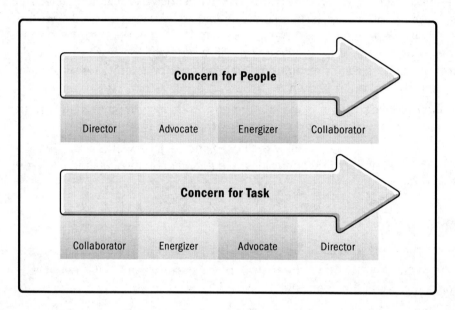

This graphic is not meant to convey that collaborators don't care about accomplishing work, and that directors are cold-hearted people that only care about work and not about the team. It's just a matter of what the leader considers first, people or task. The graphic only points to our natural inclination and how we think.

Collaborators, by their nature, think about people issues, how people will feel, how decisions will impact the team, and so forth. Energizers also consider people, but they are more likely to be thinking about how to get people excited about the task at hand. An advocate is usually removed from a lot of day-to-day interaction with the team and may not be aware of the team's thoughts and feelings. The director is focused on what needs to be done and how the team can get the work done.

As you read through the various personality descriptions you may see a description of yourself, or of people you know. Remember, this is not a description of a set way of being. It is just a model so you can evaluate your natural style and your current situation to select the best approach. The most successful project leaders have found a way to work with all approaches with ease, even though they still have a dominant style.

The Interaction between Thinking Style and Personality

After reading through the section on thinking styles and personality, you may notice that the way we think overlaps with our personality. For example, it is not uncommon for strategic thinkers to have either an advocate or energizer personality.

Advocates delegate and motivate the team, but they are fairly hands-off in their management style. This is much more consistent with thinking about the big picture rather than building a detailed schedule.

Energizers are like cheerleaders. They are compelling and enthusiastic about the vision and the possibility that a project will bring to the organization. Rarely do you see an energizer getting excited about the budget and a requirements traceability matrix!

You are more likely to see a director type wanting the control of building a detailed WBS, schedule or budget. Building the project plan is their way of communicating their expectations and insuring they will achieve their goals.

The collaborator thinks about the detailed plans from the opposite end of the spectrum. They want to work with the team to develop plans and make sure everyone is on board with the approach and can support the outcome.

Role

The final aspect of leadership styles we will look at is the role of the leader. Some situations call for more of a managerial role; others call for a more supportive role; still other situations require a role model for a leader. Your role as a leader is more flexible than your strength or your personality. You may find yourself adopting various roles at different times, or even multiple roles at the same time.

Role model. Internally, as a role model you set the example for behavior on the team. You model the behavior you want to see by upholding and reinforcing the team's values. Externally, you are the face and voice of the team. You carry the torch for the project. People evaluate the team based on your behavior and actions.

Coach. As a coach, you help your team members grow and develop. You may do this by helping them frame questions and exploring options to discover solutions. A coach can help team members gain new insights, think at a higher level and see things in new ways. Coaches may ask people searching questions to help them reevaluate their assumptions and worldviews, or to point out how certain behaviors lead to specific outcomes.

Advisor. An advisor is similar to a coach but plays more of a mentoring role. They are someone who has many years of experience and is guiding team members along the way. An advisor can be a sounding board for new ideas and can help the team work through complex and difficult problems. They are not as involved with the team as a Coach is. Many times the project sponsor fulfills the role of an Advisor.

Manager. A manager establishes the framework for the team. They establish performance metrics, track and report progress, and manage the budget and schedule. The role of the manager deals with the structure of the project work rather than the team members.

Resource manager. A resource manager is concerned with making sure the right people are available for the tasks at the right time. This role is about the logistics for the care and feeding of the team members, rather than the growth and development needs of the team members.

Enabler. This role is one that helps ensure success by removing barriers and running interference from outside influences on the team. They are also useful in helping to make decisions and solve problems.

Flexing Your Style

Just like there are some natural correlations between thinking style and personality, there are also some natural correlations between personality and roles. As mentioned previously, at any given time you may need to assume any or all roles as a team leader, so role and personality type are by no means exclusive. However, certain personality types have a greater comfort in certain roles and less comfort in others. For example, a collaborator will feel pretty comfortable assuming the roles of coach and advisor. An advocate will do well in the role of advisor and enabler. Directors are natural managers and can be good resource managers because they want to make sure they have the right person for the job. Energizers are good role models and enablers.

> **Keep in mind that the more styles you can master and the more comfort you have moving among different styles, the more effective you will be as a leader.**

In the Workplace

To help you get comfortable flexing your style in the work place, here are some tips you can use. If you are a task-oriented leader find ways to do the following:

- Work with your team to do some problem solving together.
- Find opportunities to praise good work.
- Ask questions about how the team member plans to make things happen rather than telling them what to do.
- Try and have more of a discourse in team meetings. Do more listening and less talking.
- Engage your team members to define the work they need to do. Talk through their proposed approach and fine tune if needed.

If you are a people-oriented leader, find ways to do the following:

- Engage in problem solving and project planning as a technique for getting to know the team members.
- Explore team values within the context of the project.
- Reference team member strengths as they relate to the work at hand.

Tools You Can Use

There are all kinds of ways you can assess your leadership style. I found the following web site to have a useful survey.

www.queendom.com

Reflection Exercise

Identify your strength and personality based on the descriptions provided in this chapter.

	Collaborator	Energizer	Advocate	Director
Strategist				
Planner				

Think about the roles you currently fulfill on a project are leading now, or that you recently led.

- Role model
- Coach
- Advisor
- Manager
- Resource manager
- Enabler

Do you see any areas where you should flex your personality or strength to better align with your role?

Do you see any areas where you should adopt and different role to better align with your strengths and personality?

Reflection Exercise

Sometimes our personality and the roles we play don't lead us to an outcome we are happy with. You can use the questions below to analyze a past situation and assess how you can make future situations more productive.

Think of a project management situation where your strength (Strategist or Planner), or your personality (Collaborator, Energizer, Advocate, Director) did not lead to an optimal outcome.

My Strength

My Personality

My Role

The Situation

Actual Outcome

Intended Outcome

Now think about and write down how you can flex your personality or role to improve the outcome in a future situation to lead to a better outcome.

Chapter 5

Building Your Project Team

Key Points
- High performing teams have identifiable characteristics.
- You can create an environment that fosters effective teams.
- Enrollment, engagement and shared meaning help foster a team.
- There are stages that all groups go through to become a team.

Before we talk about project teams, we need to get a working definition. There is a definite difference between a group and a team. A group of people is a collection of individuals with their own goals and agendas. They may meet periodically, but they are not fundamentally committed to the project outcome. On the other hand, a project team is a collection of people who work together to achieve the project objectives. The distinction is that teams work *together* and they are focused on achieving the project *objectives*.

For the purposes of the next two chapters, we are going to make the following assumptions:

- People want to make a difference.
- People want to contribute.
- People believe in the value of what they are doing.
- People want to apply their skills, knowledge, abilities and experience.

> "Teamwork is the fuel that allows common people to attain uncommon results."
>
> —Andrew Carnegie

Topic 1: What Does a High-Performing Team Look Like?

High-performing teams rarely occur by accident. Building a team takes deliberate effort. Team*work* involves *work*. Building a team is a process of transforming a collection of individuals with different interests, backgrounds and expertise into an integrated and effective work unit.[i]

---

[i] Vijay Verma. *Managing the Project Team* (Newtown, PA: Project Management Institute, 1997), 114.

Regardless of whether you are talking about an effective sports team, an effective production team, or an effective project team, there are certain characteristics that effective teams share.

1. **Effective teams have a shared sense of purpose.** For project teams, this is usually documented in the project charter. However, I have seen instances where the team has put together its own vision statement along with a list of team values. The collaborative effort to document a specific team vision and values helps build team cohesiveness and enhances the shared sense of purpose.

2. **There is a commitment to the team and to the individuals on the team.** Commitment to the team can be described as team spirit. Many teams have their own shortcuts and vocabulary that they use. Team members are also interested in how their teammates are doing. If one teammate seems overworked or under a lot of stress, another team member may see if there is a way to relieve their workload.

3. **There is interdependency among team members.** Team members rely on each other to get the job done. This includes an awareness of how one team member's work impacts another team member, or the rest of the team.

4. **Team members trust each other.** On a team, each team member relies on other team members to get the job done. If there are performance issues or a difference in style, team members trust each other enough to address differences in style, opinion, values and attitudes. Differences are part of project life. High-performing teams have found ways to handle differences in a way that increases trust between team members.

5. **Team members communicate openly, honestly and respectfully with each other.** Communicating openly and honestly takes trust, but it also builds trust. Therefore communicating openly is closely related to trust.

6. **There is mutual accountability between team members.** The team knows that every person is accountable for the success of the team. Therefore if a team member is not performing acceptably, another team member may challenge their performance. In some cases, the team member may need some help, in other cases their performance may just be unacceptable. Either way, effective teams hold each other accountable in a respectful manner.

7. **Teams demonstrate a high level of energy and achievement.** Teams spend their time productively aimed at the target. They are clear about what the objectives and goals are and they are focused on meeting them. This leads to achievement and fuels the energy and enthusiasm of the team. Let's face it, it is difficult to get excited about going to work to fail! But as the team stays focused on the end goal and how to achieve it together, their performance improves and their enthusiasm grows.

If you think about high-performing teams that you have seen or have been a part of, I think you will see that these teams had a clear sense of purpose, open communication, trust and respect. They held each other accountable and were willing to be held accountable by others. There was a sense of energy in the environment that was purposeful, and yet enjoyable to be around. Those are the hallmarks of effective teams.

Topic 2: Top 10 for Teams

Now that we have looked at the characteristics of a high-performing team, let's talk about what it takes to create an environment that allows teams to function optimally. As a project manager, you are a part of the team. However, a big part of your role is to establish an environment that allows the group to become a team, and not just a mediocre team, but a dynamic and thriving team. Some of the actions you take to build a thriving team are based on interpersonal skills and interactions and some are based on the management aspect of projects. Here are the top ten things you can do to enable your team to have a rich and productive experience on a project.

1. **Value your team members.** People perform better when they feel valued and respected for who they are and the contribution they make.
2. **Establish relationships.** It's not enough to value people from afar. You should establish a good working relationship with them. This is not to say you need to be best friends with your team, but you should have a decent rapport with your team members.
3. **Build trust.** Your team should trust you and they should trust each other. You can build trust by being transparent in your decision making, following through on your commitments, not making promises you can't keep, and being fair in your interactions with all team members.

"Few things help an individual more than to place responsibility upon them and to let them know that you trust them."

—Booker T. Washington

4. **Value different opinions and perspectives.** The beauty of a team is that people bring different perspectives. This allows for good discussion and usually better outcomes. Make sure you take the time to listen to varying opinions and perspectives and communicate that you appreciate and value the range of viewpoints.
5. **Define team roles.** To work effectively together, each person needs to understand their role and responsibility on the team and how it fits into the team as a whole.

6. **Communicate priorities and expectations.** For teams to win, everyone needs to understand the priorities for getting work done and your expectations. Think of this as setting the course for the work to get done, but letting the team do the navigating.

7. **Establish norms for decision making, problem solving and conflict resolution.** Three things that slow teams down and can bring them to a grinding halt are not having a structured method to make decisions, not being able to define and resolve problems, and getting stuck in a conflict situation. I will spend time with each of these in later chapters, but for now, suffice to say that you should work with your team to establish a set method to come to a decision, solve a problem and resolve a conflict.

8. **Allow for risk taking.** Create an atmosphere that allows for some risk taking and doing things outside the norm. Often, you can find new approaches and achieve better outcomes if you allow people to try something new. This also means that if the new way of trying something doesn't work out, you need to mine the lesson without blame or ridicule.

9. **Spend time in cross training, skill building and development.** Most people enjoy new challenges and growing their personal and technical skills. Find ways to help your team members cross-train to learn what other team members do. Cross-training can raise productivity when team members understand the work their peers do, and it can really save you if a team member leaves the team. You should also find out if there are skills or development opportunities that your team members want to undertake. The opportunity to learn something new can be very motivating.

10. **Appreciate your team.** Make sure you take the time to appreciate your team's efforts. Whether you are acknowledging a team member at a status meeting for doing excellent work, or acknowledging your team as a whole for meeting a milestone, appreciation and acknowledgement take very little time and make a huge impact.

> **Barriers to Team Development**
> - An environment that doesn't support team work
> - Poor communication
> - Lack of clear roles and expectations
> - Unclear project objectives, changing goals and priorities
> - Lack of team structure
> - Power struggles and political games
> - Lack of team member or senior management commitment

Enrollment, Engagement, and Shared Meaning

One aspect of creating a team feeling among team members is creating shared meaning together. Creating shared meaning includes enrollment, engagement and interpreting together. Let's look at each of these individually.

Enrollment is about presenting your team members with a possibility in such a way that the team members are interested in participating to make the possibility happen. It is about communicating in such a way that team members see the opportunity you are presenting them rather than the effort. Here are two ways to present the same information, one is enrolling, and the other is not.

Good grief! We have a project review next week! We are all going to have to do overtime and weekends to get all this work done. Better tell your family they aren't going to see you much over the next two weeks.	Okay team, all the work we have been doing for the past few months is finally coming to fruition. Our last push is to get this through the project review. I know we have all been really putting forth our best effort and I am calling you to come together to make this review the best project review this organization has ever seen. I know if we take this on together it will be a really big win for all of us.

The above scenario illustrates the point that you can create a sense of teamwork or a sense of dread, depending on your intention and the way you communicate.

Engagement is finding ways to move team members from compliance to ownership. Often, at the beginning of a project, team members complete their work because it is their job, not because they are terribly engaged in the project. However, after a time, team members start to take ownership of the project. They become *engaged* in the outcome. One of the indicators of an effective team is that they are engaged in the work they are doing. You will see this in the mutual accountability that team members hold for each other.

Team member engagement leads to higher productivity from each person and by the team as a whole. People work harder and give you that extra effort when they think their opinion and contribution will be listened to and that they matter. Engaging team members helps them find meaning in their work and they are more likely to give you that extra discretionary effort that leads to excellent work and results.

Interpreting together occurs when the team works together to figure something out, resolve an issue, solve a problem, or work through a conflict. The result is that the team helps one another reach a deeper understanding by working together collaboratively.

One way to create an atmosphere that fosters enrollment, engagement, and shared meaning is to have the team create a Team Operating Agreement (often referred to as a TOA).

Team Operating Agreement

A team operating agreement defines how the team will work together. You might also hear it referred to as a Team Charter. Team members can define the contents of the charter to meet their needs. Some of the common topics include:

- Team mission statement
- Team values

- Standards of communication
- How we communicate with each other
- Guidelines around acceptable and unacceptable behavior. For example:
  - Respecting each person's input
  - Not interrupting
  - Speaking professionally, but frankly
  - Not dominating the conversation
  - Contributing to solutions and resolutions
- Processes for:
  - Making decisions
  - Resolving conflict

Case Study

Several years ago I had the privilege to lead the project team that up-dated the *PMBOK® Guide* from the third edition to the fourth edition. When I brought the core team together for our first meeting, I set aside time to create a team charter that we would use for the project, which lasted for two and a half years. Included in the charter was a set of values, a decision-making process and a conflict management process. I won't share the entire charter, but I want to share one of the values they came up with because it was very powerful for me. The value I came to most appreciate was *"We assume each person is doing their best."* This is a very simple value, but there were times when someone was late with a deliverable, or did not turn in a status report, or committed some other project crime. My first internal reaction was to get upset. However, each time I turned to the team values, and I adjusted my thinking process to assume that the team member was doing their best. When I followed up with the person, it was always coming from a place of respect and as-suming they were doing their best. This shaped my communication and made it much more supportive and collaborative. I have tried to carry this through in my life in other areas as well, because I know it is true more often than not, and it makes communication much more productive.

Topic 3: Stages of Team Building

A classic way of describing the stages of team building and performance is the model Bruce Tuckman came up with in 1965. You may have heard of his "Form-ing, Storming, Norming and Performing" model of team development. The model represents the behaviors that groups go through from first getting to know one an-other through disbandment. You can observe these behaviors in any team, including project teams. Because this is a project leadership book, the examples I am going to give are project-based.

Forming

The forming stage is the first stage. This is the "getting to know you" stage. The forming stage may begin at the project kickoff meeting, or even before if you have been working with some team members to gather information for the project charter or early up-front planning. At this point most team members don't know each other and they know very little about the project. There will not be a lot of social interaction among the team members.

To assist team members in this stage you should provide strong leadership. In the beginning of the project you need to assert you role as project manager and make people comfortable with the project and their role on the project. Here are some steps you can take in the forming stage to successfully initiate and do high level planning for the project:

- Help team members get to know one another with an ice-breaker and introductions.
- Communicate the vision and mission of the project using a project charter, statement of work or some other document that describes the project at a high level.
- Identify roles and responsibilities associated with the project using the responsibility assignment matrix (RAM) and a high-level WBS.
- Identify authority levels and boundaries.
- Let the team develop a team operating agreement (TOA) that defines:
  o Team working guidelines and norms;
  o Decision making process;
  o Conflict resolution strategy; and
  o Problem solving process.

Storming

Remember what it was like to be a teenager, with all that emotion, uncertainty and conflict? That is like the "storming" stage of team development. In this stage team members may not be certain about their authority level, how to work with other team members, and project priorities. You can assist the team in working through this stage by adopting a facilitative style of management. This can include:

- Building trust by being authentic and emphasizing open and non-combative communication;
- Encouraging free and open sharing of ideas;
- Clarifying and facilitating the conflict resolution, problem solving and decision making processes; and
- Addressing challenges early, firmly and fairly.

Norming

In this stage there is higher-level functioning because the team focuses on problem solving and decision making, and makes better use of the relationships on the team. You are likely to see the following behaviors:

- Team member engagement
- Cohesiveness and a sense of team
- Increased productivity
- Goal oriented behavior
- Reviewing work and finding ways to improve
- Trust and respect

To optimize the "norming" stage you should adopt a democratic and coaching role to:

- Provide feedback to keep the team on track, on focus and productive;
- Continue to build good relationships;
- Continue to address areas of conflict; and
- Acknowledge and appreciate progress.

Performing

The team now has the experience of working together and uses the team knowledge and skill base to problem solve and optimize its own performance. Decision making is less stressful and more productive. Expect these behaviors:

- Mature and open communication
- Efficient and effective decision making
- Efficient and effective problem solving
- Shared leadership
- Mutual accountability
- High drive and motivation
- High productivity and initiative
- High level of team identification and loyalty
- Trust and good relationships
- Respect for differences
- Rapid conflict resolution
- Autonomy

To support this type of performance you should use a delegative and supportive style to:

- Support the team's autonomy to make decisions
- Find ways to encourage professional development
- Insure there are the appropriate challenges
- Recognize accomplishments and good behavior
- Celebrate successes

In the Workplace

When you are on a team, or leading a team, take some time out to focus on how you are performing as a team. Ask the group questions such as:

How are we working together?
What can we do better?
What are we doing well that we should do more of?

Tools You Can Use

In my experience, there aren't a whole lot of teams that are using Team Operating Agreements. You don't have to wait for the beginning of a new project to use one of these. You can develop one at any point along the way. In fact, if you have new team members, you should have them review the TOA and make sure they are in agreement with it. If you have had a lot of team turnover, you may want to take time to review the TOA and modify it to meet the needs of the current team.

Reflection Exercise

Think about a time you have been on a team that was very rewarding for you. Write down the behaviors that you noticed on the team and why they were effective. I have written an example from my past to help you get started.

Behavior	Why it was effective
A team member subjugated his goals because he thought another team member had a higher need.	It demonstrated that the team outcome was more valuable than an individual's outcome.

Now think about a time you were on a team that was either dysfunctional, or was not rewarding. Think about the behaviors you noticed and why they didn't work.

Behavior	Why it wasn't effective
I had a team leader who would get sarcastic when they weren't seeing the results they wanted.	I didn't feel valued as a team member and my motivation to perform went down.

Chapter 6

Motivating Team Members

Key Points

- Intrinsic motivation is more effective than extrinsic motivation.
- There are several motivation theories that focus on intrinsic motivation.
- There are several strategies to help you influence stakeholders.

> **"You do not lead by hitting people over the head** - that's assault, not leadership."
>
> —Dwight D. Eisenhower

Topic 1: The Importance of Motivation

Motivating team members on a project can be tricky business. For the most part, we, as project managers, are not given the authority to hire, fire, or remand our team members. In most cases, we don't even have the luxury of selecting our team members. However, we are still accountable for managing them to achieve the project objectives. Since we don't have much position power, we really need to rely on enrollment, motivation, and influence. We defined enrollment in the last chapter as presenting your team members with a possibility in such a way that the team members are interested in participating to make the possibility happen. In this chapter we will talk about motivation and influence.

If you ask people what motivates employees the first thing that often comes to mind is money. After all, that is why most of us go to work, to make money. However, salaries and bonuses aren't all that motivating. Of course you need to get paid a competitive wage for the work you do, but getting paid more is often not as motivating as meeting your own intrinsic motivation needs. Let's start by defining intrinsic and extrinsic motivation and then compare a representative list of intrinsic versus extrinsic motivating factors.

Intrinsic motivation is motivation that comes from inside the individual or is associated with the task itself. It is based on finding pleasure or meaning in the work rather than the reward.

Extrinsic motivation is performing a task based on a reward that is external to the individual.

Intrinsic		Extrinsic	
Achievement	Belief in the work	Position or title	Winning
Challenge	Self-direction	Bonuses	Pain avoidance
Making a difference		Rewards	

Research in social science has known for decades that extrinsic motivation is, for the most part, far less effective than intrinsic motivation. Extrinsic motivation works well only for a very narrow focus when there are a simple set of rules - for example, performing repetitive work that does not require much thought or creativity. However, most projects require higher cognitive skills, creative thought, problem solving and right-brain thinking. These types of tasks are more motivated by intrinsic factors.

A lot of projects require us to define problems, define solutions, find new ways of doing things, invent new technologies and innovate in other ways. This type of work is intrinsically motivated. People who work in these types of job generally enjoy the work they do. They are interested in the work they do. They like the challenge of solving problems and the achievement associated with finding new ways of doing things or inventing new solutions.

Daniel Pink, author of *Drive: The Surprising Truth about What Motivates Us*, asserts that the three main intrinsic motivators in the work environment are autonomy, mastery and purpose.

- Autonomy - the ability to direct our own lives
- Mastery - working to get better and better at something that matters to us
- Purpose - the opportunity to work in service of something larger than ourselves

These certainly aren't the only intrinsic motivators; however, they encompass a lot of what motivates the team members we work with every day. Thus, rather than providing a survey of the classic motivation theories, I am going to present the theories that are specifically focused on intrinsic factors, since they are more relevant to project team work.

Google offers their engineers "20 percent time" to work on projects they are passionate about. Many of their most successful products have come out of "20 percent time" work.

Topic 2: Intrinsic Motivational T heories

We'll start by reviewing some of the classic motivation theories are focused on intrinsic and extrinsic motivation, such as Theory X and Theory Y by Douglas McGregor, the Motivation-Hygiene theory by Frederick Herzberg, and the Acquired Needs theory by David McClelland. Then we'll move to a more modern theory, the Self-Determination Theory. We will complete this topic by looking at how over justification can impact intrinsic needs.

Theory X and Theory Y

Theory X and Theory Y were developed by Douglas McGregor in the 1960s. The theories describe two contrasting models of motivation in the work place. The theories are based on managerial attitudes, not employee behavior. A manager that follows Theory X assumes employees are inherently lazy, don't like work, and need to be constantly and closely supervised. The manager feels that employees have little ambition and need extrinsic motivating factors to keep them productive. This theory has proven to be counter-productive in most situations.

Theory Y managers assume that employees are self-motivated and ambitious. Employees enjoy their work and have the desire to be self-directed. Theory Y managers also assume employees gain inherent satisfaction in doing their jobs well and will seek additional responsibility. Theory Y is consistent with the recent research that shows most workers are intrinsically motivated.

Motivation-Hygiene Theory

Frederick Herzberg developed the motivation-hygiene theory. Herzberg's theory is based on job satisfaction and dissatisfaction. The essence is that those elements that motivate us (motivators) are intrinsic, such as challenging work, responsibility, achievement, and personal growth, result in satisfied employees. However, lack of these factors does not cause dissatisfaction. Hygiene factors are what can cause dissatisfaction. Hygiene factors include job security, salary, fringe benefits and other extrinsic factors don't bring satisfaction, but if they are missing or poorly applied, they will create dissatisfaction.

Therefore, to create the most satisfaction and the least dissatisfaction the work environment needs to provide stimulating, challenging work and maintain fair wages, good job security and decent working conditions.

Motivating Factors	**Hygiene Factors**
Cause satisfaction	*Can cause dissatisfaction*
Challenging work	Job security
Responsibility	Administration
Achievement	Fringe benefits
Personal growth	Salary

Self-Determination Theory

Self-determination theory, known as SDT, asserts that there are three inherent psychological needs that motivate people. Those needs are competence, autonomy and relatedness.

- Competence is being able to succeed in what you do.
- Autonomy is being in control of your life and acting in harmony with your values.
- Relatedness is the feeling of being connected with and caring for others.

Further research into the SDT theory has shown how certain extrinsic events can either increase or decrease intrinsic motivation. For example, positive feedback about work and results leads to an increase in the intrinsic motivating factor of competence, whereas negative feedback leads to a decrease in feelings of competence. The feedback was more effective in those situations where there person receiving the feedback perceived they had high autonomy is producing the results. Of interest is that the feedback was the most impactful when it was also linked with feelings of relatedness.

You can see how the intrinsic motivators have a synergistic effect and are stronger when they are integrated. This information is useful when you are working with your team members. Consider two different ways of giving feedback:

> One common trait that exceptional leaders embody is that they are motivated be achievemenet. Not money, not power, not recognition.

Scenario 1: Good job!

Scenario 2: You did a really great job of identifying the problem and implementing a great solution. You have really helped the team out a lot with your work and we appreciate it!

In scenario 2, each of the intrinsic motivators is addressed, and it is therefore more effective than just saying 'good job'.

These motivators aren't necessarily equally balanced. Most of us tend to have a dominant motivator. You can tailor your motivation techniques based on a team member's dominant motivating factor. Take a look at these examples:

Dominant Motivation	Approach
Competence	Set stretch goals for them to achieve
Affiliation	Make sure to recognize their achievements, especially in a public setting
Autonomy	Provide them with freedom and flexibility in their work environment, such as flex time

Over-Justification Effect

The over-justification effect is not a motivation theory; it is a pitfall that you need to be aware of. Over-justification occurs when a behavior that was intrinsically motivated is linked with an extrinsic motivating factor. Eventually, the extrinsic motivating factor becomes more important. The case study below demonstrates the over-justification effect.

Case Study

Justin is a project manager on a team that is in the *norming* stage of team development. The team has been working together for eight months and they work well together. They are even starting to do some cross-training and problem solving on their own. Justin is pleased with the team's progress, but he wants to accelerate the cross-training and autonomous problem-solving and issue resolution behavior and get the team to a *performing* stage quickly.

To encourage the team he decides to set up a reward system. Henceforth, at all team meetings Justin offers a $25 gift card to the team member who is the most helpful to other team members. He figures this will start to build a collaborative team atmosphere.

For the next six weeks, Justin employs the gift card strategy. At that point, having seen sufficient movement toward a very integrated and high functioning team he discontinues the program and calls it a success.

Unfortunately, about two weeks later Justin notices that the team is no longer showing *performing* tendencies, and in fact they are not even as effective as they were prior to introducing the reward system. What happened?

The team started behaving in a *performing* manner because they were chasing an extrinsic reward. Prior to the $25 gift card, they were working together because it felt good and it produced good results. Once the reward system was initiated, the team lost focus of the intrinsic rewards and started focusing on the extrinsic reward. Notice that the reward was really pretty small. The $25 card is not a large amount of money or a significant prize. But the $25 gift card distracted the team from what was intrinsically satisfying, and so when the extrinsic reward was taken away, so was the team's motivation.

If you want to motivate your team members, find a way to link the behavior you want to an intrinsic motivating factor. Intrinsic motivators are more powerful and last longer than extrinsic motivators.

I'll close this topic by pointing out that motivation is very personal. To be really effective at motivating your team you need to take time to get to know them individually and understand what is important to them. Some team members may be interested in a more flexible schedule, or a schedule that allows them to telecommute full- or part-time. You may have another team member that is motivated by self-improvement. You can offer the employee interested in self-improvement opportunities to cross-train or develop skills in classes and seminars.

You might want to talk with your team members about some of the information we have discussed in this book, such as finding out what their values are or what their intrinsic motivation factors are. It's fine to have the conversation candidly. That way you can align incentives with what is really important to each team member.

Some people feel it's important to treat each person the same way. Leadership, motivation, values; none of these are "one-size-fits-all." To motivate your team effectively, you need to flex your motivation to meet the needs of each team member.

Topic 3: The Role of Influencing

The difference between influencing and motivating is a subtle one. Motivating your team is more along the lines of finding incentives that cause them to want to perform. As you just got done reading, intrinsic incentives are more effective than extrinsic incentives. Influencing is more about compelling someone to take a specific action or behave in a certain way. In this section we will cover the following techniques to help you influence people.

- Provide justification
- Establish reciprocity
- Gain agreement
- Look for areas of conformity
- Identify referent situations
- Establish scarcity

Provide Justification

The first thing you want to keep in mind when you are considering how to influence someone is providing a justifiable reason why they should act or behave a certain way. The reason may be along the lines of how it will help them in the long run, or how it will support the organization or the project. People are more likely to respond in a positive manner if you state what you want them to do, and the reason you want them to do it.

For example:

> "Jim, I would really like you to put in some overtime this week because we have our customer coming next week. I really think the product needs another round of testing before we can be certain we will pass the customer walk-through."

Establish Reciprocity

Have you ever been in a situation where you are negotiating with someone and they give up something and so then you give up something? This is called reciprocity. When someone offers us something we want, we feel compelled to do something for them in return. It works best when the exchange is roughly of equal value.

"Consider this scenario:

Terri, I know you want to attend that seminar in Boca Raton next month. I can help you with that. But I need some help updating the policy manual. Would you be willing to help me with the update?"

Gain Agreement

The next step you want from Terri is her agreement or commitment to help you. Most people are compelled to honor their commitments. If you can get someone to say they will do something, they will likely follow through.

Look for Areas of Conformity

Sometimes being with a group of people that are aligned with a particular direction influences other individuals to join in. This is conformity. Taken too far, it can lead to "groupthink" where no one engages in individual thinking. Conformity is closely associated with the need for affiliation and belonging that we discussed in the section on motivation.

Identify Referent Situations

When we talk about types of power in a later chapter we will talk about referent power. That is the power and influence that comes with people wanting to be like you, or do things to please you. I'm sure you can think of times when you did something for someone just because you wanted to make them happy or make them like you.

Establish Scarcity

Finally, there is the concept of scarcity. You have probably seen commercials that say, "For a limited time only. . ." or "But hurry, we only have a few left in stock and they're going fast!" These commercials are operating on the assumption that scarcity will influence you to act - in this case, to buy what they are selling. You can influence with scarcity of time as you approach a deadline.

For example:

"The comment period for the requirements document closes in 24 hours. Make sure to get all your comments in before close of business tomorrow."

In the Workplace

Think about situations at your workplace where you can establish an intrinsic motivating factor in place of an extrinsic one. The more you can link the desired outcome with someone's intrinsic motivators, the more effective you will be. Identify some of the influence techniques you can use and apply them at work.

Tools You Can Use
Influence Table

Use this influence table to think about areas you can influence.

Situation description	Name	Influence strategy	Action
Describe the situation you need to influence	*Stakeholder you want to influence*	*Identify multiple strategies for influencing*	*Document any actions you need to take to put the strategies in place*

Team Motivation Matrix

This matrix can help you prioritize the relative importance people place on various intrinsic motivation factors. This shows five different intrinsic motivators and four team members. The motivators are ranked in relative importance for each team member. You can establish their ranking with a survey, in one on one conversation or have a meeting and talk about how each person has different perspectives on what is most important and motivating for them.

Team Member	Achievement	Mastery	Autonomy	Affiliation	Contribution
Anne	1	2	4	3	5
Beth	3	4	5	2	1
Cathy	2	5	4	1	3
Darlene	4	1	3	2	5

Reflection Exercise

1. Think about a time you were motivated. What was the intrinsic motivation?
2. Think about a time you influenced someone. What did you do or say that was effective? After reading this chapter, what techniques can you apply with your project team?

Chapter 7

Communicating is the Key

Key Points

- Effective communication focuses on the audience, not the communicator.
- Listening is a powerful communication tool.
- You can improve your ability to communicate effectively.
- There are techniques to help make difficult conversations less stressful.

Topic 1: Communication is about the Audience

As a project manager, communication is the most powerful tool you have in your tool belt. I think it's fair to say that 90% of your job is communication. Think about what you do every day:

- Facilitate team meetings
- Talk with team members
- Report on project status
- Brainstorm
- Problem solve
- Prepare project documents
- Create flow charts, schedules, diagrams, work breakdown structures, process maps and so forth

All of these activities are types of communication. Therefore, to be an effective project manager, you need to be an effective communicator. To be an effective communicator, you must communicate to your audience. I realize that sounds obvious, but think about a time you heard someone talking and you said to yourself, "This person doesn't know what he's talking about" or "She has no idea who she is talking to." The person doing the speaking had lost credibility because they did not take the time to consider their audience.

> "Constantly talking isn't necessarily communicating."
>
> —*Charlie Kaufman*

Relationship and Context

Communication is much more than just speaking or writing. The best communication is focused on the receiver of information. Being focused on the receiver starts with communicating appropriately given the relationship you have with your listener. Is that person your superior? Is it a close friend? Is it someone who reports to you? How you frame your message will depend on the answers to these questions.

The other aspect you should be aware of is the current context within which you are communicating. For example, the way you communicate in an urgent situation will be very different than how you communicate during a brainstorming session or a weekly meeting with a team member.

Focus on Reception

It isn't enough to tailor your message to your audience and the context. You should also observe how the message is coming across. This means being aware of the audience's body language, responses, tone of voice, facial expressions and so forth. Let's look at some examples. Assume Alex is talking to Tory about sequencing some of the project work scheduled for next week. First we'll see what Alex is saying, and then we'll look at various non-verbal responses from Tory.

> **Alex:** Tory, I would like to see Maryanne work on this project full time Monday and Tuesday, and then Jonathan can pick up any remaining work Wednesday through Friday. Does that work for you?
>
> Scenario 1: Tory listens to Alex, nods when he is talking and has a relaxed posture. Tory's behavior indicates that she is receptive to what Alex is talking about and engaged in the conversation.
>
> Scenario 2: Tory listens to Alex and as Alex talks her brow starts to furrow, she frowns and her head tilts to the side. This indicates that Tory is confused by what Alex is saying.
>
> Scenario 3: Tory crosses her arms, and her breathing gets more rapid. Her mouth gets pinched around the edges. Tory is indicating that she is upset about what Alex is saying.
>
> Scenario 4: Tory doesn't meet Alex's gaze. She is looking elsewhere and tapping a finger on the table indicating that she is not engaged in the conversation and is focused elsewhere.

In addition to noticing the non-verbal cues, you can listen to someone's tone of voice as they speak. You will be able to notice if they are enthusiastic, impatient, tense or in some other manner telegraphing their receptivity to the message. These techniques work best when you are face to face, since you have visual as well as auditory cues from the person with whom you are communicating. However, if you are on the phone, you can still listen to the other person and try and determine their level of engagement and interest in what you are saying.

The best way to improve your communication skills is to focus your attention on your audience, not yourself.

> "Self-consciousness kills communication."
>
> — *Rick Steves*

Topic 2: The Power of Listening

Listening can be more important than speaking. In the previous section, we stated that before you can speak effectively to an audience, you have to know who the audience is and where they are coming from. You get that information from listening.

There are three hallmarks of good listeners:

- They respect their conversation partner.
- They seek to understand the context of the situation.
- They think before they speak.

We'll look at each of these in a bit more detail.

Respecting Your Conversation Partner

To begin a conversation you need to have mutual purpose. To continue on you need to have mutual respect. I am sure you have been in situations where one person is doing all the talking; either the speaker is going on and on about how they think things should be, or they think they have all the answers. It seems no one else can get a word in. In those situations the speaker is not respecting their conversation partner.

To show respect in a conversation you should ask questions and seek information from the person you are talking with. When your conversation partner is answering, don't interrupt, but rather show interest, keep an open posture, and indicate that you are listening by nodding or encouraging them with a smile.

Even if there are behaviors and aspects of the other person you don't respect, look for some aspect that you can respect.

Understanding the Context of the Conversation

Have you been in a scenario where it seems like you and the person you are talking with should be talking about the same thing, but nothing is clicking? Frequently the reason for this is that each of you has different assumptions. Take for example the following scenario with a project team that is getting ready to launch a new version of inventory management software. The software is getting a final customer walk through next Monday and is supposed to be implemented Wednesday night. The team will spend Thursday and Friday trouble shooting.

Wendy to the team: "All right team, we have a full week ahead of us next week. We have a final walk-through, one day to make any final preparations, and then Wednesday we cut over. I need all of you at top of your game. I am sure with all the hard work we have done that this will be a relatively easy cut-over.

Linda to her teammate: "It sure will be a busy week. I have to take my son to baseball playoffs every night next week. That will make for long days."

If you are listening, you can hear that there are different assumptions about what the work week will look like next week. Wendy has an assumption that the team will be available as needed next week to work on the cut over, including after hours. Linda assumes that next week she will be taking her son to baseball playoffs every night after work hours.

Linda and Wendy are operating in different contexts in regards to importance. By listening to the underlying assumptions you can identify the difference in context early while there is time to work out a solution.

To really understand the context you should find out what your conversation partner's assumptions are. In addition, you should identify and question your own assumptions. Maybe you have those assumptions because you have never bothered to consider a different perspective. Finally, consider whether assumptions are fixed or situational. In other words, does Linda think 5:00 PM means the end of the workday and she is not open to ever working late? Or is the 5:00 PM end time based on her son's playoff schedule?

> **Tip:**
> Often it helps to ask broad, open-ended questions to deepen your understanding of the context. Here are some of my favorites:
> What else should I know?
> Is there anything else you want to say?
> What would you want to know in my position?
> What keeps you up at night?
> How can I help?

Thinking Before You Speak

You've heard the saying about counting to ten before you respond, especially when there are high emotions or there is a lot at stake. All of us have had situations where we wish we had just kept our mouth shut for a while to think about what we wanted to say, and formulate the message we wanted to communicate, rather than blurt out an emotional response. Here are some techniques you can apply to help you build better listening habits by thinking before you speak.

1. **Use silence.** Don't be afraid to let some time pass where nobody says anything. Give the conversation time to settle while you consider what to say next.
2. **Take a breath.** One way you can ensure you use silence is by stopping long enough to take a deep breath. This gives you just a bit of time to slow down before responding.
3. **Watch your conversation partner's cues.** If you are ready to speak before the other person is done talking you are missing the opportunity to watch

their non-verbal cues. We talked about those non-verbal cues in the first part of this chapter. By slowing down you can observe the other person's posture, listen to their tone of voice and respond appropriately to the context of the conversation.

> "When you take the time to actually listen, with humility, to what people have to say, it's amazing what you can learn."
>
> —*Greg Mortenson*

Topic 3: Communication Dos and Don'ts

We have discussed how important it is in communication to focus on the audience, and we have seen that in order to focus on the audience, you need to listen. Now we are going to look at some techniques to help you communicate more effectively, and some behaviors to avoid.

Flex Your Communication Style

The first thing to realize when you are communicating is that people process information differently. Generally people have a dominant sense they use for absorbing and conveying information. About 70% of us are predominately visual. That is, we absorb and process information through our eyes. To most effectively reach a visual person you should use "visual cues," or words that help them visualize what you mean. Here are a few examples:

> Help me *see* what you mean by that.
> Let me *paint you a picture* of what I am talking about.
> I can *show* you how to work with the new process.

A person who processes visually relates to words like see, picture, show, and so forth.

When you are talking to a person who processes through auditory channels you can convey the same information using different words. For instance:

> Can you *hear* what I am saying?
> Does that *ring a bell*?
> That *sounds* about right.

There are a few people who are more kinesthetic in nature. If you are talking to someone who relates more to feelings and physical experiences try some of these phrases:

> Does that *feel* right?
> That doesn't *sit* right with me.
> Let me *work* through that concept.

The most effective communicators weave in all three modes of interpreting information so they make sure to reach everyone. This is another example of where flexing your style can help you be more productive.

Communicate Responsibly

Communicating responsibly is a function of using 'I' statements and employing active listening. These skills are especially important when you are in tense situations or critical conversations.

Using 'I' statements communicates that you are taking responsibility for your own feelings, actions and behaviors. Compare these two messages:

> "I am getting frustrated because I don't think you are listening to me."
> "I'm not even going to bother talking to you because you never listen anyway."

In the first statement the speaker is taking responsibility for his feelings. In the second the speaker is blaming the other party.

Active listening entails listening to the speaker and then reflecting back the emotions, restating what they said and asking for clarification as needed. It sounds pretty simple, but it is a very powerful way to communicate. Here is an example in response to the statements above.

> "I understand you are getting frustrated because you think I am not listening to you. I want you to know that I want to hear what you are saying. Tell me what it is I am doing that leads you to the conclusion that I am not listening."

More Tips

There are times when the most effective way to communicate is to emphasize what you don't want to happen. Let's say you are working with some team members who are disagreeing about an approach to a problem. The team members are starting to get a little heated and the frustration is apparent. Rather than stating the outcome you want, in which everyone comes to an agreement and everything is wonderful, you might approach things from the opposite direction. For example:

> What I don't want is for this issue to damage our ability to work well as a team. I don't want our egos to get in the way of finding a solution we can all live with, even if it isn't the best solution for any one individual.

When you are in a conversation, or when you are facilitating a conversation you should pay attention to the environment and the team dynamics. Notice if one person is dominating the conversation, or if someone else is interrupting a

> Don't shy away from apologizing if you have done something wrong and you think it will improve the situation. An apology can go a long way in diffusing a tense situation.

lot. Make sure there is no toxic language or disrespectful body language, such as sighing, making snide remarks or being sarcastic.

Communication Barriers

Now let's look at some thought patterns that present barriers to communication and then look at behaviors that inhibit authentic communication.

Stereotyping, making assumptions and thinking you already know the answers are thought patterns that present barriers to true communication. Consider the following scenarios.

- **Stereotyping.** Stereotyping is counterproductive when someone thinks all people of a certain group think or act a certain way. For example, "Everybody knows that engineers will over-architect a system. You have to manage them really tightly or they will over run your schedule and budget with features that nobody wants."
- **Assumptions.** Making assumptions without bothering to validate them can lead to misunderstandings and lack of effective communication. We often assume that people understand and interpret things the way we do, but this is rarely the case. Take the time to check in with your team members to make sure everyone has a consistent understanding of the situation.
- **Perceived omniscience.** Thinking you already know the answer, and that the person you are speaking with has nothing of value to contribute, is a barrier to communication. In the first place, the person communicating feels disrespected and will often withdraw. Secondly, the listener loses out on gaining insight and knowledge from the speaker.

"Assumptions are the termites of relationships."

—Henry Winkler

Communication Inhibitors

In the book *Crucial Conversations*,[i] the authors talk about silence and violence as unhealthy patterns in communication. Silence can entail masking, avoiding or withdrawing.

- Masking is selectively showing our true opinions. Sarcasm is an example of masking. Consider the following: "No problem! We can meet that more aggressive timeline even though you have reduced our resources by 20%. It'll be a walk in the park!" The real message is that there is no way we can meet the deadline, and you have sabotaged the project.

---

[i]Patterson, Grenny, McMillan, Switzler. *Crucial Conversations* (Place: McGraw Hill, Year) page number.

- Avoiding is steering the conversation away from the sensitive subject.
- Sponsor: "I think you should include another round of verification testing for next week."
- Project Manager: "Did I tell you the new status reports are really working well? They are a lot easier to fill out."
- Withdrawing is pulling out of the conversation altogether - for instance, saying you have another meeting you need to attend or a phone call you have to make.

Silence patterns basically inhibit communication by not addressing the problem. On the other hand, violence patterns attempt to convince, control, or compel others to adopt a particular point of view. Controlling, labeling and attacking are violence patterns.

- Controlling includes dominating the conversation or forcing your opinions on others by not letting them be heard. This can include exaggerating, using absolutes and twisting the facts to meet your needs. Here is an example:
  "We used that risk management stuff before and all we did was waste all kinds of time with absolutely no results!"
- Labeling is similar to stereotyping that we talked about above. It is putting a label on people or ideas so they are dismissed under a general stereotype.
- Attacking includes threats and belittling such as, "If you make me look bad again in a staff meeting it'll be the last staff meeting you'll attend at this company!"

Some of the violence examples may seem a bit intense. Violence can be more subtle than depicted here, but the results are the same. The person communicating intimidates and bullies others to get their way.

Topic 4: Challenging Conversations

One of the more difficult aspects of communicating is having challenging conversations. A challenging conversation is one that can have significant emotion, or when the stakes are high, or when the parties have opposite opinions. Here are some situations that can result in challenging conversations.

- Addressing substandard performance by a team member
- Poor product, project or performance quality
- A team member who is consistently behind schedule
- A team member whose work is consistently over cost
- Inappropriate behavior in meetings
- Putting a team member on warning
- Firing someone or releasing them from your team due to poor performance

- Addressing a team member who is not keeping their commitments
- Working with a functional manager who is not providing promised resources

Secrets for Success

Turning a challenging conversation into a successful conversation can be a daunting task, but if you follow these steps, you will find that it is easier than you thought.

1. Get clear on what you really want. Ask yourself what you want for yourself, what you want for others, and what you want for the relationship out of the conversation. Think about the bigger picture than the position you are holding. Think about the long-term solution you want. Sometimes it helps to clarify the outcome you want by thinking about the outcome you don't want.

2. Create a safe environment that allows all parties to communicate relevant information openly without fear of reprisal or ridicule. This means that all parties can share feelings, opinions, ideas, and concepts, even if they are controversial or unpopular. You can't have a free flow of feelings and opinions when the environment of sharing is not safe. It isn't the content of the message that makes people feel unsafe; it is the environment or condition of the conversation.

   Let's say you work in an office environment. Set aside some time where you can both sit down with the door closed and when you won't be interrupted by colleagues, phone calls, texts, emails and so on. When you sit down, keep an open posture, don't lean into the conversation, keep your voice conversational and try to keep your breathing deep and even. By setting up your body language this way you are accomplishing two things: first you are telling your brain that things are okay and relaxed. Second, you are communicating a relaxed, open environment to the person you are talking with.

3. Come from a place of collaboration. Focus on *and* not *but, or, etc.* When you are focused on 'winning' or being right your brain chemistry adopts a fight or flight environment. Your blood and adrenaline goes to your muscles. However, when confronted with a complex problem, such as how to create a win/win situation, the "and" instead of the "but/or", the blood goes to your brain to work on the solution.

4. Establish common ground. This can be as simple as articulating the big picture solution, such as "I know we want to make the best decision for the project, and even though we see things differently, I believe we want to be able to find a successful resolution and avoid hard feelings."

5. Don't go into silence or violence. Avoid the non-productive communication patterns we talked about earlier. Instead, continue to create a safe environment by being honest and keeping your intended goals at the forefront of your mind.

Following these five steps doesn't mean that every challenging conversation you have will turn out wonderfully. After all, you can't control how other people approach the conversation. However, by adopting this model you will increase your effectiveness in challenging conversations.

Communicating for Improved Results

We can use the information for challenging conversations and add a few extra steps that will bring all the previous information in this chapter together and give you a 10-step model for addressing performance issues.

1. Be clear on the intended outcome. Just like challenging conversations, you need to be clear about the intended outcome you want.
2. Gather all relevant facts (do not rely on hearsay or rumor). Before talking about performance, make sure you do your research and know the facts. Don't use gossip and hallway conversations as a basis for a performance conversation.
3. Establish a safe environment. Conversations about performance can definitely fall under the 'challenging conversation' classification. Therefore you need to establish a safe environment where both of you can talk openly and honestly.
4. Clarify the gap between expectations and results. If you have documented roles, responsibilities, and acceptance criteria documented, use those documents to clarify expectations. Contrast the expectations with the actual results based on the facts you have collected.
5. Use non-judgmental language. Don't use accusatory language, such as "You always. . ." or "What were you thinking when. . ." Using "I" statements helps keep the language non-judgmental.
6. Watch both your own and the other person's body language and tonality. Earlier in this chapter we talked about focusing on reception and how the other person is receiving your message. Make sure to observe the non-verbal cues to see how your message is coming across.
7. Do not get sidetracked into a defensive mode, past situations, justifications, or other's performance. Stay focused on the outcome you want. Don't let the person you are talking to sidetrack you with other issues. This is avoiding behavior that we covered in the Silence or Violence topic.
8. Be empathetic, but firm. It is good to be empathetic, but you still need to be firm about your expectations.
9. Establish a plan for improvement. Make sure you have concrete steps in place to reach your intended outcomes. Don't leave the meeting without understanding exactly how the person is going to improve performance and meet your expectations.
10. Set a follow-up meeting to evaluate the progress. Use the follow-up meeting to fine tune the improvement plan or to acknowledge the performance improvement.

Case Study: Addressing Poor Performance

Here is a fictional case study of a challenging conversation that addresses poor performance.

Drew and Freda are about to have a conversation about Freda's recent performance on the job. Freda is a long-term employee who has performed reasonably well over the years. However, recently her work habits have deteriorated. She has had to rework a number of deliverables and is causing the project to overrun the critical path.

Before Drew talks with Freda he thinks about the outcome he wants. He knows he doesn't want to put Freda on probation, but he also wants to see immediate and significant improvement in her performance. He is interested in what is causing the recent deterioration in performance, but will respect her privacy if she does not volunteer a reason.

Drew wanted to have the relevant facts prior to his meeting with Freda so he did some research to identify when Freda's performance started to deteriorate and discovered that about four months ago Freda started missing deadlines. Prior to that time everything seemed okay.

When Freda arrives at Drew's office he asks how she is doing and sits back to listen. He keeps his posture open and listens to what she is saying, but also how she is saying it. He notices that throughout the conversation Freda periodically looks distracted and that she will sometimes close her eyes and her mouth pinches together. Drew interprets this as a sign of stress. So he asks her, "Freda, it looks to me like you are anxious or stressed about something. I notice that recently your work has not been up to your usual standards and that you have needed to rework some deliverables. I'd like to know what is going on so I can see if there is a way I can help you get things back on track."

Freda responds by saying "Well, you know, John was late with a deliverable last week and I don't see him in here getting reprimanded." Drew maintains his open posture and does not get into a defensive mode. He remembers the outcome he wants, which is an immediate and significant improvement in Freda's performance. So he says, "I appreciate your point, but right now we need to focus on the fact that in the past four months your performance has not been up to your usual level. I want to talk with you about that and find out what we can do to improve your results."

At this point, Freda reveals that her mother-in-law's health is ailing and that she has moved in with Freda's family. In addition to work Freda has been trying to care for her mother-in-law, find a more permanent solution and balance the needs of her family. She states that her husband has stepped down to working 32 hours a week at his job so he can provide

(continued)

Case Study (*Continued*)

more care, but Freda really needs more time at home, just in case there is an emergency.

Upon hearing this Drew shifts into problem-solving mode and the two of them work out a performance improvement plan that includes moving Freda to a 4-day, 40 hour a week schedule so she can have an additional day at home to help with the family care situation. They decide to meet again in a month to see if the new hours help get Freda's work performance back on track.

While this is a fictional scenario, you can see how Drew used all techniques necessary for effective communication. In addition to deploying the techniques for challenging conversations, he also made sure to gather the facts, watch for non-verbal cues from Freda and himself, and established a plan for improvement. See if you can recognize each of the following 10 steps used in the Communicating for Improved Results section:

1. Be clear on the intended outcome
2. Gather all relevant facts (do not rely on hearsay or rumor)
3. Establish a safe environment
4. Clarify the gap between expectations and results
5. Use non-judgmental language
6. Watch yours and the other person's body language and tonality.
7. Do not get sidetracked into a defensive mode, past situations, justifications, other people's performance, etc.
8. Be empathetic, but firm.
9. Establish a plan for improvement
10. Set a follow up meeting to evaluate the progress

In the Workplace

Use the listening techniques described in this chapter to focus on the audience for your communication. Pay attention to the verbal and non-verbal cues to see if your message is coming across as intended.

Use active listening skills, such as paraphrasing or asking clarifying questions to insure you are receiving messages as intended.

Avoid the communication barriers and inhibitors. If you see a co-worker engaging in those types of behaviors, use the techniques for challenging conversations by establishing a safe environment and establishing a common ground to talk about the situation rationally.

Don't shy away from challenging conversations. Practice the techniques discussed in this chapter to build a level of proficiency. It really does get easier with practice.

Reflection Exercise

Think about how you have used conversation inhibitors from the silence or violence topic. Think about a specific situation where you adopted those behaviors. Identify what you're anxious about, or why you were trying to protect yourself. See if you can find a way to make the environment safer with the person you were talking to so you can both have a productive conversation without employing the silence or violence behaviors.

Chapter 8

Managing Your Team

Key Points

- Critical thinking helps you make the best possible decision in a given set of circumstances.
- Having a defined problem solving model can help keep you on target.
- Making sound decisions requires a structured, analytical approach.
- There are techniques to having effective meetings.
- You should evaluate the team's performance on a regular schedule.
- Toxic behaviors can be contagious; therefore, you need to know how to address them.

In chapter 1 we looked at the most important project leadership skills. Problem solving was identified as the number one most important skill in project leadership, and decision making was number four. In this chapter we will discuss both of those skills. Before doing that we need to take a look at critical thinking. Critical thinking plays a large role in solving problems and making decisions.

Other aspects of managing your team are making sure your meetings are effective, evaluating the team performance and addressing toxic behaviors in a timely manner. We will discuss each of these in the latter pages of this chapter.

Topic 1: Critical Thinking

Critical thinking is the ability to make the best possible decision under a given set of circumstances. This means applying reasoning that is free from bias and personal feelings. As a project manager, there may be many times when you may feel pulled to make a decision without all the information, or when you think you can overcome obstacles that you can't. These biases, which we discuss more a bit later, can hinder you from making the best possible decisions.

There are, of course, times when you need to make a decision under conditions of uncertainty. Sometimes, regardless of the information or data you have, there is no clear best answer. In this case you will need to employ judgment. It is always nice to have sufficient data to make a decision, but if you don't have that, you will need to rely on your judgment.

The information in this section will help you to distinguish between data, which is objective, and interpretation, which is subjective. If we aren't aware of fallacies in our reasoning or our own personal biases, we can easily mix up fact and opinion, thereby making decisions that are not optimal. We'll start by looking at some key definitions used in logic and critical thinking and then identify some fallacies and common biases, wrapping up with a brief discussion on the power of questions.

Inductive Reasoning

When we talk about critical thinking we use specific terminology. For example, in critical thinking an "argument" is a set of data or facts (called the premises) that are offered in support of some conclusion. Most of our day-to-day reasoning is through inductive arguments or reasoning. Arguments take a particular form called the structure of the argument. First, you outline the premises and the chain of logic, and then you assert the conclusion. An inductive argument is structured in such a way that if the premises are true then the conclusion is *likely* true, but not necessarily.

Inductive arguments are frequently based on statistics or past behavior. If something has happened frequently in the past, it is likely that without a change in the facts, it will continue to happen in the future. The more it has happened in the past, the more likely it is to happen in the future. We can use inductive reasoning when we are building cost and duration estimates for our project. The example below is constructed as an argument for developing a duration estimate.

> Premise 1: This project requires that we obtain a county permit.
> Premise 2: The last 12 times we got a permit it took between 15 to 18 days.
> Conclusion: The duration estimate of 18 days is sufficient time to obtain a county this time.

You can see how the premise of requiring a county permit and the information on how long it has taken the last 12 times builds a compelling argument for 18 days to be a sufficient estimate for this time. In reality, this is *likely* sufficient time, but it's possible that it might not be enough time.

The way assess if an inductive argument is a good argument is by looking at the following:

- The form of the argument is structurally sound. In other words, the the there are one or more premises that lead to a conclusion.
- The data or premises are true.

- The chain of logic is clear and reasonable.
- The conclusion logically follows the chain of reason offered in the premises.

The example of the duration estimate is structurally sound and the premises are based on fact. There is a clear and reasonable chain of logic and the conclusion follows the chain of reason offered in the premises. However, remember, this only means that it is a strong argument, not a fact. There are times when strong arguments don't end up with the intended outcome.

Here is an example of an argument that is not structurally sound.

> Premise 1: To take the PMP all project managers must have either a college degree and 4500 hours of experience directing and leading projects or a high school diploma and 7500 hours of experience directing and leading projects.
>
> Premise 2: To be a PMP all project managers must pass a 200 question exam.
>
> Conclusion: All project managers with the appropriate experience pass the 200 question exam.

In the example above, the premises are true, but the conclusion does not logically follow the premises, because there many people with the experience who do not pass the exam, and many people who could pass the exam without the experience.

Reasoning Fallacies

The above descriptions seem pretty logical. Unfortunately, as human beings, we aren't always logical. Some of the more common reasoning fallacies include:

- Appealing to emotion rather than reason as the basis for an argument
- Assuming the premise is true if the conclusion is true

Let's look at each of those a little closer.

Appealing to emotion rather than reason as the basis for an argument. Appealing to emotion can take the form of moving towards positive emotions or away from negative emotions.

If you have ever bought a new car, you know the sales person wants to play on your emotions. They want you to love how the car drives, the new car smell, and all the cool new gadgets. Many times that feeling of buyer's remorse shows up after you have made the emotional decision to buy the new car and the reality of the payments hits you!

An example of avoiding negative emotion can be not disclosing to your boss that you are behind on your schedule. It is logical to disclose the information as soon as possible so you can get help while you can still recover from the variance. However, sometimes we want to avoid the feeling of failing to hit our targets, or disappointing our boss, so we will not say anything until we absolutely have to, and often it is too late to do anything about it at that point.

Assuming the premise is true if the conclusion is true. Sometimes we agree with the conclusion or outcome of a decision and we then infer that the argument or premise is true. For example, your manager may ask you to deliver on a milestone a week early. It just so happens that you had built in some lead time for a customized component and it arrived early. Therefore you are able to meet the new delivery date. Absent the information about the early component delivery your manager may come to the conclusion that by asking for deliverables early, he will get them early and can therefore accelerate the schedule.

Biases

Biases are related to fallacies in reasoning. A fallacy is faulty logic. A bias is a mindset that can cause faulty logic. There are two types of biases, cognitive and motivational. Cognitive biases are a deviation in judgment because of how the human mind is wired. Think about an optical illusion. Your mind knows what it seeing can't be real, but your eyes still show it to you.

Motivational biases are a deviation because of how a situation affects us. There are many different types of motivational biases. Below are some of the more common ones.

1. **Peer pressure.** Peer pressure can cause us to make decisions or behave in ways because we want to be accepted by our friends and coworkers, even if we don't necessarily think what we are doing is the best decision.
2. **Confirmation bias.** Confirmation bias means searching for and interpreting information in a way that aligns with our own pre-conceptions. Another aspect of a confirmation bias is framing or presenting information in a way that reflects our own personal experiences. You may see this as selective listening or people hearing only those things that they want to hear or that are consistent with the way they see the world.
3. **Illusion of control.** The illusion of control is thinking you can control or influence outcomes that you can't - for example, thinking that your team will be willing to work overtime to meet a deadline or conversely thinking your powers of persuasion will cause a sponsor to extend a deadline.
4. **Avoiding uncertainty** We will tend to gravitate towards a solution that reduces or eliminates uncertainty because we are not comfortable with the unknown.
5. **Ignoring probability.** Sometimes we get the crazy idea that even though the odds are against us we can overcome them and the situation will work out

in our favor. Sometimes it does. But in reality, the odds are the odds and they don't change because we want them to.

6. **Anchoring your decision on one data point.** Making a decision based on one instance of an occurrence is not generally a good idea. It is better to have more robust data and experience making a decision.

7. **Authority bias.** An authority bias is agreeing with someone in a real or perceived position of authority. Sometimes we think that because a person has position power, a big title, or an advanced degree that they must be right. This is not always the case. We should apply solid reasoning regardless of a person's title or education.

8. **Availability of data.** Relying on data that is easy to attain does not always lead to a well reasoned decision. Sometimes it is the data that is difficult to attain that is more accurate. The availability of data is related to believing data that is repeated often. Just because someone tells you frequently not to worry, they will meet their deadline, does not make it true.

9. **Projection.** Projection is assuming others share a similar thought, belief or value as you. Projection can be difficult to detect because we often can't see our own beliefs and how they may not be true.

So how do we avoid falling into faulty reasoning or being subject to biases? Well asking questions is a good place to start.

Questioning

Asking questions is a good way to validate your thinking and your logic. However, there is an art to asking good questions. Keep these four tips in mind when you are asking questions:

1. **Purpose.** The question should move you forward towards either developing better reasoning, a better solution to a problem, or a better decision.

2. **Accuracy.** The question should be relevant to the issue. It can be easy to get sidetracked by questions that are slightly off topic so you need to make sure the question pertains to the problem or decision at hand.

3. **Precision.** Make sure the question is at the appropriate level of detail. Often times people will ask questions that are "down in the weeds" when the big issues are still undecided.

4. **Clarity.** Good questions should bring about mutual understanding. In other words, the answer to the question should help your team see things in a more aligned fashion.

Now that we have a common understanding of critical thinking, we'll take a look at how it applies to solving problems and making decisions.

Topic 2: Problem Solving

Solving problems is the most important skill a project manager brings to the table. And let's face it: projects are fraught with opportunities to solve problems! Whether it is trying to get the project done faster, with less funding or with changing resources, all of these situations require problem solving skills. Fortunately there is a relatively straight-forward seven-step model you can use to help methodically solve problems.

1. **Define the situation or problem.** The most important step, and frequently the most difficult, is clearly defining and concisely articulating the problem that you are trying to solve. It is important to work with your team, or with others who are trying to solve the problem, to ensure you all have a common understanding and a clear grasp of the problem you are addressing.

2. **Identify the outcomes you want to achieve.** Once you have defined the problem you need to identify what outcomes would resolve the problem. Without clearly understanding acceptable outcomes you won't be able to make the best choices among possible solutions.

3. **Select the criteria you should use to make the decision**. If there are certain criteria you need to meet or consider when making the decision, you should identify those criteria. If there are multiple criteria it may be appropriate to rank them in importance.

4. **Brainstorm solutions.** Once you have done all the pre-work of defining the problem, identifying the outcomes and selecting the criteria you can start to brainstorm solutions. Remember, brainstorming should be a free flow of ideas without applying any of the criteria. Brainstorming is a creative process that is used to generate as many options as possible.

5. **Compare solutions to criteria.** Once the brainstorming has stalled, you can start to compare the various options to the criteria you selected. Many of the options will get weeded out in this step. What you are left with is a set of possible solutions.

6. **Identify any risks, issues or negative consequences associated with each of the possible solutions.** Some of the possible solutions might introduce new risks or issues or they might exacerbate existing risks or issues. After this step is complete you should have at least one viable solution.

7. **Select the best option.** If you have more than one solution, select the one with the highest likelihood of success and the least cost and effort to employ. It is fine to rank the other options for fallback options if needed.

The following case study shows how the problem solving model can be applied on a project.

Case Study

The Diodex project has been steadily falling behind schedule for the past six months. At this point, the project manager has called together a group of team members to help solve the problem.

Anthony, the project manager, gives the following information.

"Ever since we started the design phase of this project we have been steadily falling behind. We are currently 3 weeks behind on the critical path and we are coming up on a project review. The technical work on this project is not all that challenging, so that is probably not what is causing the problem."

Anne, the system engineering team lead, says, "Well, we are fully resourced, but most of the designers have been out of school less than five years and they are pretty new to the company. There have been several times when they have taken longer to complete their work than a more experienced designer would take and they have made some mistakes that set the timeline back due to rework."

Bill, the resource manager, states that the original estimates were based on the assumption that all team members would have at least 5–10 years experience and an average skill set and productivity rate.

Anthony says, "I think we can frame the source of the problem as the fact that the people doing the work are different from the people who estimated the work and that the skill sets and expertise is less than estimated. This allows us to state the problem as 'Due to inexperienced team members work is taking longer to complete.' Is that correct?"

The team agrees with the problem definition and moves into defining the outcomes they want to achieve. Based on a brief discussion they identify the following outcomes:

1. Regain 2 weeks of the schedule slip

2. Identify a way to eliminate any future schedule deterioration

Bill says "I want to make sure that part of our solution criteria involves upgrading the skills of these team members and does not include any disciplinary action. I think these are good team members, they just need help furthering their skills." Anne adds that she needs to make sure all the policies and quality checks remain in place. Brian, the finance officer for the project, states that he is comfortable releasing some money from reserves, but that he can't release more than $12,000 to get the schedule back on track.

The team discusses the criteria and ranks it as:

1. All quality policies must be followed

2. The solution cannot use more than $12,000 in reserve

3. Team members get help improving their skill set

(continued)

Case Study (*Continued*)

Once this is done the four start brainstorming solutions. They continue doing this for about 20 minutes and come up with a number of possible options. As they compare each option to the solution criteria a number of them are discarded because they go outside the quality criteria, or are cost prohibitive. What they are left with is the following possible solutions:

- Bring in 2 outside designers for 3 weeks
- Reassign the existing resources to a less critical project and bring in more advanced designers
- Bring in a team lead with extensive experience to do work and mentor the designers

These solutions are evaluated for risks and other negative consequences. Based on the current status of the project the group determines that reassigning the existing resources and bringing in a more advanced team would put the schedule further behind and would leave the feeling that the existing resources had failed. It would also not help the existing resources improve their skills.

Based on the two remaining solutions the group decided to bring in a team lead with extensive experience to accomplish some of the more challenging work and to help the existing design team find ways to work smarter and faster. They decided to hold off on bringing in outside designers for the time being but agreed to re-evaluate that option if there was not substantial schedule improvement in the next two weeks.

> **Brain Tip**
>
> Your brain wants to learn and be challenged. Your brain works most creatively when it is relaxed and in a predictable environment. When there is safety and security, the brain can deal with the challenges of problem solving—i.e., the areas of the brain that are higher functioning. To insure your team is productive in a problem-solving session you should send out an agenda and a strategy for the problem solving session. This allows people to come in knowing what is expected and access the higher levels of their brain for creative and imaginative thinking.

Topic 3: Decision Making

It may seem counter-intuitive to say that good decision making is not measured by the outcome, but it is true. Generally, a good decision-making process leads to a good outcome, but not always. For example, the decision to use a more skilled resource and pay more to accelerate the schedule may be a good decision; however, if a higher priority project comes along and that resource is reallocated, the outcome may not be as optimal as if you had chosen a less skilled resource in the first place.

How do you know you are making a good decision? Well, one way is you can see if the decision has the following elements:

- The decision is based on critical thought and reasoning as much as possible
- The risks are clear to all stakeholders
- The decision makers put the decision above their own interests

If all these things are true, you are on the way to making a good decision. There are two types of decisions you will be faced with, veridical and adaptive decisions.

- Veridical decision making is based purely on facts. You should use veridical decision making for technical decisions.
- Adaptive decision making is based on fact and prior experience or emotions. Use adaptive decision making for leadership decisions.

Adaptive decision making includes considering the following variables:

- The environment the decision impacts
- The individuals the decision impacts
- The priorities of the organization and the project
- The possible consequences of the decision

For both veridical and adaptive decisions you should employ good decision-making techniques. The following model will help you through the process.

Decision-Making Model

You may notice that some of the steps in this model are similar to the problem solving model we covered in the previous topic. That is because solving a problem and making a decision both require critical thinking and higher brain functioning than other types of activities you will perform as a project manager.

1. **Define the decision accurately, clearly and precisely.** Similar to problem solving, you need to be able to clearly articulate the decision you are making.
2. **Define criteria to evaluate data and the course of action.** Criteria for decision making can include risk vs. benefit, chance of failure vs. success, ease of implementation, and so forth.
3. **Challenge assumptions.** Before you make a decision you should look to see the assumptions you and others have around the variables associated with the decision. For example, you may decide to use heavy duty construction materials assuming that what you are building will have lots of traffic and will need to be functional for seventy years or more. It would be a good idea to challenge the assumption, or at least question it, to make sure before spending the extra funds associated with heavy-duty construction materials.

4. **Ensure the data you are using to help make the decision is reliable and credible.** This is related to challenging assumptions. To make a good decision you need to have reliable data. Your decision is only as relevant as the data you base it on.

5. **Brainstorm options.** Like problem solving, you should consider various decisions and their likely outcomes.

6. **Apply criteria.** Once you have numerous options for decisions, you should evaluate how well they meet the criteria you established in step 2.

7. **Select best option.** The best option is the one with either highest probability of success or highest payoff (or the least probability of failure or lowest risk)

As you go through the decision making process you will need manage the environment and the team. You should pay particularly close attention to managing the following items:

- **Manage bias.** Make sure that none of the biases identified in the critical thinking section are tainting the decision making process

- **Manage uncertainty.** People are uncomfortable around uncertainty. Do your best to introduce certainty where you can.

- **Manage group dynamics.** Making difficult decisions can sometimes bring out the worst in people. Make sure you are managing the dynamics to keep the process constructive.

Tips for Making Good Decisions

To make good decisions follow these tips:

- **Keep the big picture and the system in mind.** Don't forget that almost every decision you make will have an impact on some other aspect of the project, on another project, or on the operations of the organization.

- **Recognize your own bias and the bias of others.** Make sure that neither you, nor the others involved in the decision, are operating out of either self-interest, or their own biases (as outlined in the section on critical thinking).

- **Keep an open mind.** You may end up with a decision that you had never even considered, or one that is completely new to you. That's fine. Be willing to adopt new options.

> **Brain Fact**
>
> Decision making is handled by the prefrontal cortex. The prefrontal cortex considers various aspects of decisions, looks at the options and then makes a choice. It combines emotions from the amygdala and rational thought. A lot of the processing in the pre-frontal cortex is subconscious.
>
> Dopamine also plays a role in decision making. It inhibits unnecessary and unwanted thoughts from the focus of the problem, and it remembers what works and what make you feel good in the past as well as what did not work and led to feeling bad in the past.

- **Challenge assumptions, not people.** One of the steps in the decision making model is to challenge assumptions. However, make sure it is the assumption you are challenging, and not the person who holds the assumption!
- **Interpret and analyze data logically by separating facts from opinion.** Decisions need to be based on facts, not opinion. Apply critical thinking and good reasoning to insure you are analyzing information logically and accurately.

Topic 4: Holding Effective Meetings

Meetings can be very productive, if managed correctly, or a complete waste of time. One of the most common complaints I hear is that people meet repeatedly, but nothing gets accomplished. Another common complaint is that nothing gets done because people are always in meetings and have no time for work.

The basic ground rules around meetings are:

- Publish an agenda prior to the meeting, and follow it
- Manage the group to stay on topic and on time
- Have an action item list and follow up on it
- Publish meeting minutes within 48 hours

The above are very basic meeting management tips and likely you have heard the information before. To take your meetings up a notch you can increase participation by sharing control, increase retention by paying attention to how you deliver the message and you can take the opportunity to build a more cohesive team.

Sharing Control

Your team will participate in meetings more if they have an opportunity to engage in the planning and managing the meeting. Here are some simple ways you can engage your team:

Before the Meeting

- Send out the agenda early and give people an opportunity to identify additional items they want to include, or delete unimportant items
- Share the responsibility for bringing snacks, managing the meeting logistics and taking notes

During the Meeting

- Be deliberate in getting feedback from people, especially those that seem to be unengaged or silent
- Get input on decision making criteria
- Ask for the best way to approach talking through items, or problem solving a scenario

After the Meeting
- Take the meeting temperature and ask for input on how to improve effectiveness of meetings in the future
- Get feedback anonymously

Increase Retention

Let's face it, meetings can be dry. If we aren't actively engaged we can forget much of what is said. So how do you increase memory retention? The following tips should help:

- **Restate the information in a few different ways.** Not everyone will relate to what you say in the same way. If you really want to impart the information clearly use different communication styles. In chapter 7 we discussed that people process information differently. You can relate the information to visual, auditory and kinesthetic cues to make sure you are referencing each person's dominant style.
- **Use facts and examples from real life to make a point.** Wherever possible use real life scenarios to relate to the information. Give examples of when a specific problem or risk occurred and how it was handled. The examples can have positive or negative outcomes. The point is to give people something to which they can relate.
- **Use stories or metaphors to make a point.** If you don't have a real-life example you can use a story or a metaphor that demonstrates the point you are trying to make.
- **Add emotion and humor.** People remember emotion. The emotion can be enthusiasm, urgency, passion, or anything else. If you tie the emotion to the message people are more likely to remember the message. You can also use humor. Humor releases dopamine and makes people feel good. Wouldn't it be great if people left meetings actually feeling good!
- **Create a visual display.** As mentioned previously, most people process information visually. Use white boards, flip charts, on-screen presentations or any other method of creating an image. You can use images to show a process flow, create a bullet list of follow-up items, create a parking lot of open items, or any other method of getting information exhibited for participants to see.

Building Relatedness

You can use your meetings as a way to create more of a team feeling. To increase feelings of relatedness it is best to have face-to-face meetings. However, in today's business world, many of our team members are in different locations, so face to face meetings aren't always possible.

One way to build relatedness is to create your own logos, code words, short cuts and so forth. It creates a sense of bonding to have a team name and logo, or to have inside jokes and expressions. As the team leader you can initiate some of this, but much of it needs to grow from within the team. Stay alert to opportunities to build off of your team's past experiences together to build stronger bonds in the present.

In between meetings you can keep the communication open with email updates, blogs, intranets and IM technology.

Topic 5: Team Evaluation

Part of managing your team is checking in with team members individually to see how they are doing and evaluating the team as a whole. When you check in with team members individually you should not only address their specific work and performance, but you should also talk about how they are performing as a team member. Are they contributing? Are the detracting? Are they feeling included and recognized? Or are they feeling like they don't make a difference? Having time with each team member to see how they are feeling about the team as a whole provides a safe environment to flush out issues about team dynamics that might not otherwise be addressed.

When you are evaluating your team performance you can compare it to the information we covered in Chapter 5 about high-performing teams. The call out box has a summary of characteristics of high-performing teams.

Characteristics of High-Performing Teams
- Shared sense of purpose
- Commitment to the team and individuals on the team
- Interdependency among team members
- Team members trust each other
- Team members communicate openly, honestly and respectfully
- There is mutual accountability
- High levels of energy and achievement

Other behaviors to look at to evaluate team performance include:

- Is the team meeting the project objectives?
- Are team actions consistent with the values in the team operating agreement?
- Are they using the team operating agreement to resolve their own conflicts and issues? (The team operating agreement is described in chapter 5).
- Are people working together and are they enjoying it?

If you feel your team is demonstrating effective behavior, that's terrific. If there are some areas that can use improvement, take a look at how you can facilitate improved performance. You might want to revisit the information in Chapter 5 on creating an environment that fosters effective teams (see *The Top Ten for Teams*) and make sure they are engaged in the process.

Topic 6: Dealing with Toxic People

Emotions are contagious. If you have someone on your team that consistently brings the mood down, or is irritable or apathetic this behavior can spread to other team members. Everyone is entitled to a bad day, so don't worry about negative behavior if it is a rare occurrence. However, if the behavior is consistently toxic or negative you need to address the situation with the team member.

Common toxic behaviors include:

- Gossiping
- Unconstructive criticism
- Drama queen or king
- Bitterness
- Constant complaining
- Blaming others

Open and honest communication is the first step in addressing the behavior. Perhaps there was a specific event, person or condition that led to the toxic behavior. If this is the case, have a frank discussion with the person about the situation and see if you can defuse the negative emotion associated with it. If the behavior is more ingrained, then you need to let your team member know the impact their behavior has on other team members in a tactful way. Make sure you can point to specific examples of what was said and the impact of those statements. If the situation gets too personal you may need to get assistance from a human resource professional.

Tools You Can Use

Below are some tables that you can use to track your decisions and plan to increase retention in meetings.

Decision Log

Decision description	Criteria	Selected solution	Comments
We need to select a vendor for a key component in our new product. The choice is between Vendor A, who has a higher price and a proven on time delivery, or Vendor B, with a lower price but an unproven delivery record.	Vendor must be on the approved list Vendor must be able to deliver early or on time	Vendor A	For this project, time is of the essence and the delivery is on the critical path. Vendor A has a 95% on-time delivery record, whereas Vendor B is a newer vendor without sufficient data to determine the on time delivery reliability. Therefore we chose Vendor A.

Meeting Planning

Agenda item	Example or fact	Story or humor	Visual aid
Change in sign off process for quality reviews	Cite the duration range that it takes from the time quality reviews are scheduled to when they are finalized and signed.	Describe the situation with Alpha Corp where the sign off on the quality review took 5 weeks, caused a delay in meeting a phase gate deadline and ended up with a very irate customer.	Show a diagram of the old process and the new process.

Reflection Exercise

1. Think of a time when you or your team needed to make a complex decision.
   - What was the experience like?
   - Did everyone have the same understanding of the decision?
   - Was the process organized?
   - Was the result of the decision favorable or unfavorable?
   - What information from the decision making topic could you have applied to the process to make the decision making process easier?

2. Think of a situation where you witnessed a team member displaying toxic behavior.
   - Describe the behavior
   - Describe the impact
   - If you were going to have a conversation with the team member today, how would you address situation?

Chapter 9

Leading Virtual Teams

Key Points

- Virtual teams have different challenges than in-place teams.
- The skills needed to effectively lead virtual teams are somewhat different than those needed for managing in-place teams.
- The behaviors needed to lead virtual teams are similar, but there are some key differences.

Leading a project is difficult enough, but when your team is distributed across multiple sites, time zones, countries, or cultures, it can be very challenging indeed. Leading a virtual team requires the same leadership skills and behaviors as leading an in-place team (or on-site or co-located team); however, the relative importance of particular skills and behaviors is quite different.

In this chapter we will look at the challenges of managing a virtual team and the skills and behaviors that are most effective in leading virtual teams.

Topic 1: Why Virtual is Different

In addition to the usual challenges involved with leading a project, virtual teams bring specific challenges associated with being in various locations and sometimes having different languages and cultures with which to operate. We'll take a look at some of those challenges and some techniques you can use to overcome them.

Challenges Associated with Virtual Teams

The most prevalent challenge associated with virtual teams is that virtual team members may not feel a sense of being part of the team. This can be especially true if the majority of the team is in place and only one or two team members are virtually located. Often the off-site team members feel like they are an afterthought. When team members don't feel they are really a key part of the team, they may not feel enough relatedness to openly and honestly express their views and opinions. This leads to further feelings of isolation.

In addition to the reduced feeling of inclusion on the team, there are other challenges:

- On virtual teams there is a reduced ability to pick up non-verbal cues. We talked about non-verbal cues in Chapter 7. This can lead to misunderstandings and misinterpreting the conversational context.
- Different cultures and languages can easily lead to misunderstandings and miscommunications, especially around colloquial phrases.
- Working in different time zones can make it difficult to get everyone together for a meeting. If you have an overseas team member or members, they may be up in the middle of the night to attend meetings.

While these challenges are real, there are also some actions you can take to help reduce the impact and severity of distributed team members.

- Spend time getting to know each person individually
- Encourage people to share openly and honestly
- Consider assigning some distributed leadership
- Invite people to share personal sides of themselves
- Encourage people to connect outside of team meetings

For multi-lingual teams, you should also consider the following:

- Use simpler terms and define what you mean if you think the words can be misinterpreted
- Ask for feedback from team members and listen for indicators of understanding or misunderstanding
- Speak clearly and concisely
- Allow more time for discussion and clarification of language and understandings

For teams with representatives from different cultures you should also:

- Allow each team member to share their values
- Create team values that are global enough to include all team members

Topic 2: Virtual Behaviors

In chapter one I mentioned that PMI conducted a survey of project managers from 66 different countries to determine the skills and behaviors that are most influential in delivering projects successfully. About 75% of the respondents had worked on a virtual team. The top seven behaviors needed for a successful virtual team were ranked as:

- Collaboration
- Cultural sensitivity
- Openness, transparency and authenticity

- Facilitative
- Reliability
- Decisiveness
- Assertiveness

As you will notice, many of the most influential behaviors are same the between virtual and in place teams, thought their ranking may be slightly different.

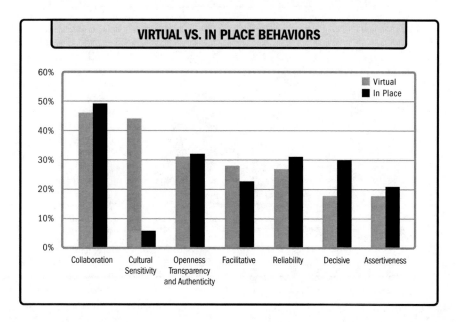

For both virtual and in place teams the most important behavior is collaboration. The only significant difference is the importance of cultural sensitivity in a virtual environment. Cultural sensitivity is the number two most important behavior in a virtual team. For in place teams it is number thirteen! The difference is clearly reflective of multi-cultural, widely distributed teams.

Topic 3: Virtual Skills

Unlike the relative similarity in behaviors between virtual and in-place teams, there is a significant difference in skills that make a project manager effective in virtual environment versus an in place environment. Communicating a compelling vision is important for both types of teams, as is team building. However, other than that similarity, there is a wide disparity in skills. The most important skills for leading teams in a virtual environment are:

- Communicating a compelling vision
- Written communication
- Active listening

- Team building
- Establishing a clear vision
- Oral communication
- Coordinating and balancing conflicting interests

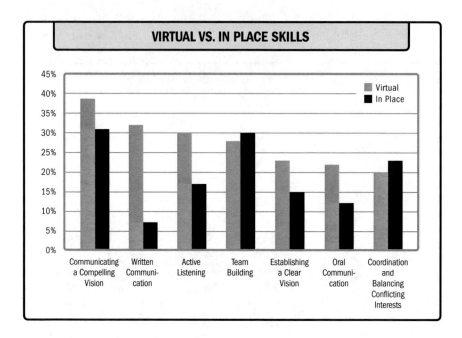

As you can see, there is an emphasis on communication for virtual teams. Therefore make sure you build in the extra time necessary for communicating both verbally and in writing.

In the Workplace

When you are leading a virtual team, make sure you spend extra time and attention on developing a complete communications management plan. In addition to the regular fields, a virtual communications management plan should include, at a minimum, the stakeholder, their primary language, and their time zone.

Tools You Can Use

VIRTUAL COMMUNICATIONS MANAGEMENT PLAN

Project Title: _____ Date Prepared: _____

Stakeholder	Primary Language	Time Zone	Message	Medium	Frequency

Acronyms	Definition

Communication Constraints or Assumptions

Attach relevant communication diagrams or flow charts.

Chapter 10

Managing Conflict Effectively

Key Points

- Conflict is normal on projects. How you handle it can determine whether it is constructive or destructive.
- There are many sources of conflict on projects, and the likelihood of a particular cause of conflict changes over the lifecycle of the project.
- There are five general approaches to resolving conflict. Knowing the five approaches and the best time to use them gives you options to choose from.
- Having a model to resolve conflict can help you to approach conflict in a healthy way.

Topic 1: The Nature of Conflict

Conflict happens, especially on projects! Projects are fraught with uncertainty, tight timelines, lack of money or resources, and frequently, in the beginning, a limited understanding of the scope of the project. All these factors lead to a stressful environment and therefore an environment that is ripe for conflict.

Conflict is a natural state of affairs in projects and it is inevitable. Therefore, it is worth your time to understand that conflict doesn't have to be a negative experience. There are actually some positive outcomes associated with conflict. For example, conflict:

- **Challenges the status quo.** People get to experience different ways of viewing a situation. In many cases a new way of doing something arises out of a conflict.
- **Gets people involved in problem solving.** You can treat a conflict like a problem that needs to be resolved by applying the problem solving steps we talked about in Chapter 8.
- **Minimizes group think.** Many times when a team works together over extended periods of time they start to think alike and they adopt repetitive behaviors and patterns. This adaptive behavior isn't necessarily bad, but it can be beneficial to challenge the status quo and identify different patterns of thinking.
- **Deepens team relatedness.** When the team works through conflicts and problems together it increases the team relatedness and improves the group dynamic among team members.

Of course, conflict can also have negative repercussions. For example, conflict can:

- **Kill team spirit.** If conflict is not managed constructively team members may become so distant and dysfunctional that they won't want to interact with others on the team.
- **Reduce communication.** When conflict exists we often shut down and stop talking or engaging.
- **Cause team members to withdraw.** Many people are conflict-avoidant. In other words, they will take actions to remove themselves from the conflict, including withdrawing, either from the team or from the situation.
- **Reduce trust and the amount of risk people are willing to take.** Often in conflict situations team members will lose trust in their team mates. Reduction in trust also reduces the amount of risk a team member is willing to take, either in the project or among project members.
- **Build animosity and factions.** Reduction in trust can lead to negative team behavior such as building factions or cliques. This behavior can negatively impact team cohesiveness and performance

How can you help foster the good aspects of conflict and reduce or minimize the negative impacts? For openers, try these four steps.

1. **Use open communication to resolve conflict.** Often times when we are in a conflict situation we stop communicating, either because we don't feel safe communicating or because we develop apathy towards the situation ad stop caring about the outcome. Whatever steps you can take to open up dialogue between the parties experiencing conflict will help the situation.
2. **Focus on the issues, not the person.** Remember, the conflict is about perceiving situations differently, it is not personal. Keep your behavior respectful while you work to resolve the issue at hand.
3. **Focus on the current, not the past.** Stay focused on the current issue rather than thinking about similar situations that have occurred in the past. You may be frustrated because you have engaged in similar situations previously with either the same person or someone else. Bringing up those past situations won't help you resolve the current one; it will only add fuel to the fire.
4. **Search for alternatives together.** By looking for resolutions and alternative solutions together you can actually help repair any damage the conflict has caused and create a more constructive relationship. In addition, by working together you can generate more options and more creative options for resolution.

Topic 2: The Evolution and Sources of Conflict
The Evolution of a Conflict

Conflict evolves through a series of steps before it turns into an argument. It starts as an internal dialogue, evolves into physiological reactions and then grows to external dialogue. By understanding the evolution of a conflict you can learn to spot it in the early stages and intervene before it becomes really contentious.

The first phase is a degradation in your internal dialogue. For example, you may find yourself thinking "This person is always so hard to deal with" or "Oh great, here we go again." If you are aware of your internal dialogue at this phase you can intervene fairly easily by adjusting your attitude before the situation escalates. Try changing your internal dialogue to something along the lines of "I think we are going to be able to work together to resolve whatever issues we have."

If you are not able to change the internal dialogue, the next point of escalation is physiological reactions. Physiological reactions encompasses non-verbal cues. During this phase the body is getting ready for a fight. The autonomic nervous system is kicking into the fight-flight or freeze mode. You may notice a change in breathing rate, facial expressions, or tone of voice. At this point, to intervene you need to do something to address your physical reaction. You can try leaning back in your chair and relaxing your posture or taking several deep breathes, slowing down your rate of speech and deliberately talking softer. All these steps tell your body that there is nothing to fear and your body stops sending fight or flight chemicals into your blood stream.

The final step in conflict escalation is when the internal conflict is externalized. This means that you might notice that you are making emotional decisions and statements or that the volume of your voice has increased. You are probably upset and feeling anxious, scared or angry. At this point, your best option is to take a time out. Taking some time away from the situation allows you time to return to a neutral state and think more rationally.

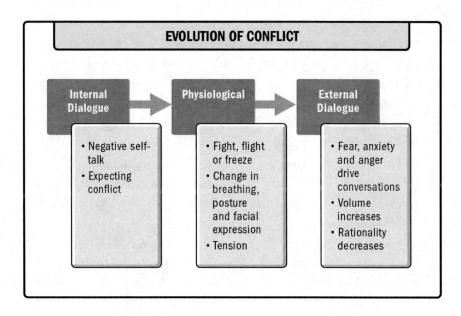

EVOLUTION OF CONFLICT

Internal Dialogue
- Negative self-talk
- Expecting conflict

Physiological
- Fight, flight or freeze
- Change in breathing, posture and facial expression
- Tension

External Dialogue
- Fear, anxiety and anger drive conversations
- Volume increases
- Rationality decreases

Sources of Conflict

In 1975, Hans J. Thamhain and David Wilemon studied the sources of conflict on projects. Much has changed since their study, but project management has not changed all that much. While the technology has changed, and many more organizations have developed a level of maturity in managing projects, the sources of conflict are still relatively stable.

1. Schedules
2. Priorities
3. Human resources
4. Technical issues
5. Cost
6. Administrative issues
7. Personality

The project **schedule** and all its component parts is the number one source of conflict, regardless of the phase in the project lifecycle. Schedule conflicts include differences of option on estimates, sequencing of activities, uncertainty about the work effort required, and even the correctness of the schedule model being used.

Priorities about project work are a frequent point of contention. Team members associated with designing a new product will have different priorities than people who are going to market the new product. Priorities can also impact the development approach and lifecycle selection.

Availability of **resources** can be one of the most difficult challenges to deal with on a project. Most projects are understaffed, or don't have the optimal skill sets in house. Therefore the project manager may need to negotiate with functional managers as well as other project managers.

Conflict associated with **cost** can stem from cost estimates, trade-offs on costs associated with the project versus life cycle, maintenance costs, and distribution of funds.

Technical issues are generally about the product and can include performance trade-offs, ways to resolve defects, and quality assurance activities.

Administrative issues are associated with the structure of the project - for example roles, responsibilities and reporting relationships. They can also be associated with the management style and project management activities such as the frequency and types of meetings.

Personality issues are based on how team members get along with each other and how they interact. Personality issues are usually relatively easy to resolve because most people in the work place understand the need to work together and behave professionally.

As the project moves through the project lifecycle you are likely to see the frequency and intensity of conflict shift. Towards the beginning of the project, during the chartering and early planning activities, most of the conflicts will be centered on priorities. You may see some administrative conflicts as team members push back on the number and types of meetings, the reporting relationships and their role on the team.

During detailed planning, you will start to see more conflict around schedules, resources, and technical issues. When you are developing or executing the project the schedule, resources, technical issues, cost, and priorities are all fair game for a conflict.

Project closure brings a flurry of schedule conflict as everyone tries to complete their work on time with the resources available. By now the priorities and human resource, technical and administrative issues have all been resolved. As mentioned previously, personality issues are not all that difficult to resolve, and they can show up at any time in the project life cycle.

Topic 3: Thomas-Kilmann Conflict Resolution Model[i]

The most widely known conflict resolution model is based on work done by Ralph Kilmann and Kenneth Thomas. The model measures behavior in conflict situations based on two dimensions: assertiveness and cooperation. In other words, the extent to which a person attempts to satisfy his or her own concerns (assertiveness) and the extent to which a person attempts to satisfy the needs of others (cooperation) are the primary traits measured Based on these two dimensions, there are five modes for resolving conflict: competing, accommodating, avoiding, collaborating, and compromising. We will look at each of these in greater detail.

1. **Competing** is a behavior that is assertive and uncooperative—an individual pursues his own concerns at the other person's expense. This is a power-oriented mode in which you use whatever power seems appropriate to win your own position—your ability to argue, your rank, or economic sanctions. Competing means "standing up for your rights," defending a position which you believe is correct, or simply trying to win.

2. **Accommodating** is a behavior that is unassertive and cooperative—the complete opposite of competing. When accommodating, the individual neglects his own concerns to satisfy the concerns of the other person; there is an element of self-sacrifice in this mode. Accommodating might take the form of selfless generosity or charity, obeying another person's order when you would prefer not to, or yielding to another's point of view.

3. **Avoiding** is a behavior that is unassertive and uncooperative—the person neither pursues his own concerns nor those of the other individual. Thus, he

[i]Thomas, K.W., and Kilmann, R.H., Thomas-Kilmann Conflict Mode Instrument (TKI), Mountain View, CA, 1974.

does not deal with the conflict. Avoiding might take the form of diplomatically sidestepping an issue, postponing an issue until a better time or simply withdrawing from a threatening situation.

4. **Collaborating** is behavior that is both assertive and cooperative—the complete opposite of avoiding. Collaborating involves an attempt to work with others to find some solution that fully satisfies their concerns. It means digging into an issue to pinpoint the underlying needs and wants of the two individuals. Collaborating between two persons might take the form of exploring a disagreement to learn from each other's insights or trying to find a creative solution to an interpersonal problem.

5. **Compromising** is a behavior that is moderate in both assertiveness and cooperativeness. The objective is to find some expedient, mutually acceptable solution that partially satisfies both parties. It falls intermediately between competing and accommodating. Compromising gives up more than competing but less than accommodating. Likewise, it addresses an issue more directly than avoiding, but does not explore it in as much depth as collaborating. In some situations, compromising might mean splitting the difference between the two positions, exchanging concessions, or seeking a quick middle-ground solution.

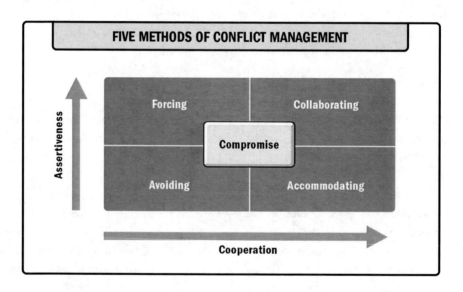

Each of us uses different modes based on the situation. It is another way that we flex our leadership style. We tend to have a dominant mode, one we feel most comfortable with, but we can access the other modes as needed. The following table outlines the five modes of conflict resolution and some situations where each mode can be most effective.

Mode	Situation
Competing	When you need to make an unpopular decision When you need to act immediately When the stakes are high If the relationship is not important *Be aware that this is usually not an effective long-term method. You should only use this method after other methods have been tried.*
Accommodating	To reach an overarching goal To demonstrate open mindedness and flexibility To maintain harmony When any solution will be adequate When you will lose anyway To create goodwill
Avoiding	When you can't win When the stakes are low If you need a cooling off period To preserve neutrality or reputation If the problem will go away on its own
Collaborating	When there is time and trust When the objective is to learn When you have confidence in the other party's ability Useful in multi-cultural situations When you need a win-win solution
Compromise	When both parties need to win When an equal relationship exists between the parties in conflict To avoid a fight

Topic 4: Steps to Manage Conflict

The seven steps below provide a framework for managing conflict. Collaboration and compromise are usually the most effective methods of resolving conflict and thus this framework assumes those modes of resolution.

1. **Clearly articulate the conflict.** You should be able to state each party's position and perhaps the source of the conflict as well. You can't work on resolving the conflict until both parties are clear on the point of disagreement.
2. **Identify rules of engagement.** It is a good idea to set out the rules of engagement, such as not referencing past conflicts, being disrespectful, interrupting, or taking statements out of context.
3. **Identify what a successful outcome looks like.** Think about what you want out of the conflict resolution. You may not need to both be thrilled with the solution. Perhaps you can agree to settle on a resolution that doesn't meet all your desires, but also doesn't go against any of your key values.

4. **Understand the implications of not resolving the conflict.** There may be situations when time will take care of the situation.
5. **Brainstorm solutions and resolutions.** Similar to problem-solving, you should brainstorm and discuss various options to resolve the conflict. There is frequently more than one way to come to resolution.
6. **Identify any risks, issues or negative consequences with possible solutions.** Sometimes you may find a solution that both parties can live with, but it introduces down-stream risks or problems. Make sure you understand the possible repercussions of each potential resolution.
7. **Select the best option to resolve conflict.** Given what you identified as a successful outcome, and the risks and issues associated with the various solutions, select the best resolution strategy.

The conflict resolution modes and the framework can help make it less uncomfortable and improve the likelihood of a positive outcome in conflict situations.

In the Workplace

Challenge yourself by getting outside your comfort zone . Many people are uncomfortable confronting a conflict situation, or being accountable for making a tough decision. Use these opportunities for personal growth.

Tools You Can Use

You can plan how to address a conflict by filling out this simple table to help you organization your approach.

Description of conflict	Intended outcomes	Conflict resolution style	Next steps

Reflection Exercise

Think of a time when you were involved in a conflict.

- What type of resolution style did you use?
- Was the style appropriate to the situation?
- Was the outcome satisfactory?
- Given the information in this chapter, is there anything you would do differently now?

Chapter 11

Advanced Topics

Key Points

- There are different types of power that you will employ as a project manager.
- Building trust is an essential ingredient in leading your team.
- Men and women think differently. Understanding gender differences can help you lead your team more effectively.
- There are scales that can help you understand your team members' temperaments and personality.
- Technology has impacted the way we act and the skills of our team members.

Topic 1: Power

Power enables leaders to influence team members, functional managers, peers and other stakeholders. As project managers we have various types of power, depending on the project manager, the organization, the project, and other factors. It is important to understand the different types of power and how they are derived. We will look at four different types of power:

- Formal or position power
- Expert power
- Reward/penalty power
- Referent power

Formal/Position Power

Formal/position power refers to the positions in an organization such as Manager, Vice President, Director, Supervisor, and others who have power derived from their position. A project manager has a certain degree of power derived from a project charter that authorizes him or her to apply organizational resources to accomplish a project. This is also known as legitimate power.

Expert Power

Expert power is based on a person's talents, such as skills, knowledge, abilities, or previous experience. This is generally the type of power team members have. They are subject matter experts in their particular area. Though there are people who out-rank them, their opinions usually are given significant weight in decision-making.

Reward/Penalty Power

Reward/penalty power is the ability to assist someone in getting what he or she wants, or to withhold what he or she wants. Reward power includes recognition, money, skills, and input into performance evaluations. Penalty power may include the ability to censure someone or to assign less desirable work. Penalty power is sometimes called coercive power. Typically, if you have formal power, you also have reward and penalty power.

Referent Power

This is power because people want to work either with the project manager or on the project itself. An example would be wanting to work on the Olympics because it is such a well-known and exciting project. Referent power may also include power derived from "who you know." For example, if you golf with the CEO of the organization every Saturday, you may have referent power because of your relationship with him or her.

More on Power

Some references discuss other types of power such as information power (what you know) and charisma power (power associated with your personality). In the model I described above, I consider information power to be a subset of expert power and charisma power to be associated with referent power.

As a project manager, you will need to flex your power. You may have a certain degree of position power depending on your organization's org chart, the relative importance of the project you are working on, or the project charter. Depending on your background, you probably bring some kind of expert power with you from a technical area. However, the longer you spend as a project manager, the more likely you will lose technical expert power and gain expert power as a project manager.

Your reward and penalty power is highly dependent on organizational policies with regards to staffing and HR issues. Referent power can be based either on your personality (charisma) or the relative importance of the project to the organization. Learning how to leverage each type of power, as appropriate and needed, is the key to flexing your power.

Topic 2: Building Trust

The one thing you can do to make your job as a leader easier is to build trust with your team. If your team members, your sponsors, your customer, and your peers trust you, they are more likely to communicate openly and participate in decisions, problem solving and conflict management, as well as actively engage as part of the team.

Like the other aspects of leadership we have covered in this book, there are specific actions you can take to build trust with your team.

1. **Make and keep agreements.** If your team members, sponsors, customers and peers (stakeholders) see that when you commit to something you follow through, they will trust your word. To make it easy to keep agreements, make sure you are specific about what you are committing to. For example, if someone wants to meet with you soon, set a date and time. Soon is not specific and you may have a different interpretation about what soon means than the other person. It goes without saying that you should not make agreements you cannot keep. However, if you find yourself in a situation where you can't keep your agreement, communicate as soon as possible and then make a new agreement that you can keep.

2. **Find common ground.** As human beings we tend to trust people that we think are similar to us. If you can find areas of common ground you will find it easier to build a trusting relationship. Common ground can include common goals (such as those articulated in the project charter), common hobbies or backgrounds, similar education, or past experiences.

3. **Cite history.** It is logical that future behavior will be consistent and similar to the recent past. If you are looking to establish trust with someone, point to past behaviors that indicate you are trustworthy. Conversely, if you are assessing whether or not you can trust someone, look to their past behaviors.

4. **Openness and transparency.** People trust people who are open and don't hide their interests and agendas. The more open you are the more likely people are to trust you. In Chapter 2, we talked about knowing yourself and being authentic by living consistent with your values. Knowing your values, and acting in a way that is consistent with your values, are both good measures of your openness and transparency.

By practicing these behaviors you will start to exhibit trustworthy behaviors and consequently to build trust. Trust is a goal to strive for. It may take a while to build it. Continue to work towards it, and over time you will notice that you have acquired it.

Topic 3: Gender Differences

Men and women think differently. Some of those differences may be accentuated by the environment and the way we are raised. However, there is a definite physiological component to the way we think. Men's and women's brains are wired differently.

Brain Mechanics

Men have nearly seven times more gray matter in their brains than women do. Gray matter is used to focus on a single task and target. It is about staying focused on the task at hand and getting the job done. Therefore, men tend to be more task oriented and results driven than women.

In contrast, women have ten times more white matter in their brains than men do. White matter is used to integrate information from various parts of the brain. It connects different parts such as memory, emotion, and speech. Because women are better at integrating information from multiple sources they tend to think about and focus on relationships more than the tasks.[i]

The task orientation versus relationship orientation starts very young. Young boys remember things, whereas young girls focus on people. This is not to say that men don't see emotions; they do. They just use a more primitive area of the brain. The primitive area is more reactive and engages the fight or flight response. On the other hand, women are more reflective. Women integrate information from tone of voice, body language, mood, and other communication cues.

> **Brain Fact:**
> Males speak about 7000 words a day, compared to females 20,000.

When you are working with male team members you will be more successful if you communicate the outcome you want and allow them to figure out how to achieve it. With female team members it is helpful to start out by establishing a connection, whether by small talk or through shared experiences. This reinforces your relationship before discussing the work that needs to be accomplished. Female team members may want to discuss the approach they will take with you and get your feedback on their ideas. The sense of collaboration makes women more comfortable.

Gray matter and white matter aren't the only physiological differences; women get 15–20% more blood flow to their brain than males do. Women's brains are active throughout the day and don't require rest. On the other hand, male brains require rest to perform.

Compete vs. Collaborate

Men are designed around competition and the desire to win. This is a result of the testosterone in their bodies and the adrenaline and cortisol that get released under stress. Adrenaline and cortisol prepare the body for fight or flight. Therefore, on a chemical level, men get ready to argue and defend their position.

Conversely, when women are under stress they release adrenaline and cortisol like men, but they also release oxytocin and serotonin. Oxytocin is a bonding chemical. It makes people feel close to each other. Serotonin is a calming chemical. This leads women to want to collaborate and cooperate under times of stress.

---

[i]Marilee Sprenger. *Leadership Brain for Dummies*. Wiley Publishing, Inc., Indianapolis, Indiana. 2010.

Leveraging the Differences

What does all this mean to you as a leader and how can you use this information to enhance your team's performance? Having the team work together to set project goals and the approach to pursuing those goals together works well. It allows for male testosterone for motivation and dopamine and oxytocin for increased bonding. The target will motivate the men and the team working together for a common goal will motivate the women. The overall sense is a feeling of team identification and team work. There is intrinsic motivation because of the feel-good chemicals and extrinsic rewards in achieving the goal.

Topic 4: How People Think

Brain chemistry can explain some of the differences in the ways we think, but there are other parts of our makeup that are better described as our "personality." One of best-known models for categorizing personality types was first developed by the well-known psychiatrist Carl Jung. Jung's work was expanded by Katharine Cook Briggs and her daughter, Isabel Briggs Myers. Their work is known as the Myers-Briggs Type Indicator, or the MBTI. It is taken by over one million people every year and is one of the most prevalent personality instruments ever.

There is a broad array of information on the MBTI and it would be a disservice to try and cover it all here; therefore, I will only present a brief summary. Should you wish to find out more there are many publications and web sites that have additional information.

MBTI Relating Styles

The four scales in the MBTI are:

Each variable has an abbreviation:	
Extrovert = E	Thinking = T
Introvert = I	Feeling = F
Sensing = S	Judging = J
Intuition = N	Perceiving = P

- Extroversion and Introversion
- Sensing and Intuition
- Thinking and Feeling
- Judging and Perceiving

We'll look at each of these scales a little closer.

Extroversion and Introversion. This scale looks at how we are energized.

Extroverts are energized by interaction with the external environment. They are activity-oriented and like to be where the action is. They are often gregarious and don't mind being the center of attention. These people are good in brainstorming sessions because they like to think out loud. As a leader you can appreciate the collegial atmosphere that extroverts create; however, don't let them dominate the situation at the expense of other team members!

Introverts prefer to be reflective. They are interested in thoughts and ideas rather than activities. An introvert wants to think things through before sharing their ideas.

They are comfortable staying in the background. As a leader, make sure you give introverts time to process before asking them to participate. However, don't overlook them just because they are quiet! Often, their reflection leads to good ideas and outcomes.

Sensing and Intuition. This scale looks at how we prefer to absorb information.

People that are sensing absorb information through their five senses. They are pragmatic and concrete. They are interested in the facts. A sensing person will want to know the data, scoring methods, or other quantifiable information about a situation. They tend to be very focused on the present, not the past or future. As a leader you can count on the sensing people to keep the conversation grounded in the present and on track.

Intuitive people absorb information by looking at patterns in data and implications and meanings of the patterns. They want to understand the big picture and have a context to hold information. Intuitive people can think abstractly and are likely to have insights based on looking at patterns in information. You can utilize intuitive people to understand future implications of current information and to analyze trends in data.

Thinking and Feeling. This scale looks at how we prefer to make decisions.

Thinking people make decisions based on logic and rational thought. They look at data and make a decision based on the odds or economic implications. You can count on your thinking people to have a solid understanding of the costs and benefits associated with various options on your project. They will weigh the alternatives and make a decision based on the best possible outcome given the available data.

Feeling people are more likely to make subjective decisions based on their concern for people. They evaluate their values, feelings and beliefs before coming to a conclusion. As a leader you can count on these people to raise concerns about how a decision will impact other people. They are the team's conscience.

Judging and Perceiving. This scale looks at how we deal with the outside world.

Don't confuse the term "judging" with being judgmental. In the context of the MBTI, a judging person is one who deals with the outside world by having a goal orientation and a structure to achieve those goals. They are good at time management, planning, and organization. Sounds a bit like a project manager! Judging people are good at presenting information in a straight forward, organized manner. They like order and are usually on time and prepared for their meetings.

Perceivers like to keep their options open. They are flexible and are able to respond to changes in the project and the environment easily. If they are project managers they probably follow a more agile approach, rather than a traditional project lifecycle.[ii,iii]

[ii]Steven Flannes and Ginger Levin. *Essential People Skills for Project Managers* Vienna, Virginia: Management Concepts, 2005. 43–50.
[iii]James Lewis. *Project Leadership.* McGraw Hill, 2003. 28–32.

The following table is a high-level summary of the information above.

Extravert or Introvert	
Extravert	Keeps energized and stimulated by lots of contact with others and the outside world
Introvert	Receives energy from time to reflect on internal thoughts or ideas
Sensing or Intuition	
Sensing	Attends to the world through a concrete, pragmatic approach. Real time focus
Intuition	Wants to look at the big picture, considering possibilities with a future-time orientation
Thinking or Feeling	
Thinking	Decisions are made based on an analytic approach, stressing the facts
Feeling	Decisions are made based on personal values, emotions and other subjective concerns
Judging or Perceiving	
Judging	Operates by creating a plan or agenda; strives for closure on a task
Perceiving	Likes a minimum of structure; strives to keep options open and stay flexible

Reprinted with permission from *Essential People Skills for Project Managers* by Steven W. Flannes and Ginger Levin. © 2005 by Management Concepts, Inc. All rights reserved. www.managementconcepts.com.

The four types combine into sixteen different combinations. But remember, this is just a model to explain and categorize personalities. The four scales are relative, they are not fixed. In other words, we are not one way or another. If you are an introvert it doesn't mean you never enjoy being around people. There are degrees of introversion and extroversion, and the situation you are in will influence all of the behaviors in the scales. The model merely represents a preference or how you relate the majority of the time.

MBTI Temperaments

Sixteen types can seem a bit overwhelming. Dr. David Keirsey looked at the combination of how we communicate and how we use tools. Communication has to do with how we use words. Some people use concrete words and examples and others are more abstract. Concrete communicators are precise and sensory oriented. Abstract communicators talk about ideas and concepts, such as fairness, or beauty.

How we use tools is about whether we are likely to use tools cooperatively or in a utilitarian way. Using tools cooperatively means the way society 'expects' them to be used. For example, you should use a hammer to drive a nail home. Using tools in a utilitarian way indicates that if it works, use it, regardless of what people think or what the intended use would be. For example, a rock can work as well as a hammer to drive the nail home.

By combining the communication and tool use variables, we can see four basic temperaments.

- Idealist (NF Intuitive-Feeling)
- Rational (NT Intuitive-Thinking)
- Guardian (SJ Sensory Judgment)
- Artisan (SP Sensory Feeling)

Idealists are abstract communicators and are cooperative in their use of tools. They believe in ideas and ideals and they are consistent with the rules and expectations of society.

Rationals communicate abstractly and are utilitarian in how they use tools. They believe in ideas and ideals and are willing to be unconventional in achieving their goals. These people can solve problems by thinking differently and creating innovative solutions. You will see a lot of engineers and inventors with this temperament.

Guardians communicate concretely and use tools cooperatively. A lot of managers are guardians. They are fond of policies and procedures and like to have an agreed-upon process.

Artisans communicate concretely and use tools in unconventional ways. These are very artistic people and don't tend to fit in well in corporate environments. They are more likely to be craftsmen or artists.[iv]

Understanding how your team members communicate and use tools can help you to communicate more effectively and see where and why there are likely to be conflicts on your team. You can take steps to leverage your team members' temperaments with the type of work they do and the way you monitor their progress.

Topic 5: The Effect of Technology

I'll wrap up this book with a brief look at the effect of technology on how we work. As we develop technology that enables us to get things done faster and more efficiently, we adapt our skills and thinking patterns to this faster pace. This is most obvious in a group now commonly labeled the "digital natives." Digital natives grew up with cell phones, the internet, CDs and other tools. This group is always electronically connected. However, because of this, they are chronically distracted and almost always multi-tasking. It can be said they have continuous partial attention and don't focus on one thing.

Some of the benefits the digital natives bring to the team include the ability to get information quickly, communicating across cultures, and good problem solving

---

[iv]ibid. 32–35.

skills. On the downside, they have a short attention span, fewer people skills, and a lack of skill in reading body language.

On the other side of the spectrum are the digital immigrants. These are the baby boomers and older people who rely more on paper information. They also don't have the ability to skim information as quickly as the digital natives. However, they have the wisdom and experience to engage in complex tasks like problem solving, strategy, forecasting, and predictions, and they can see the consequences of actions.

The digital immigrants have better people skills, are good listeners, and are more experienced in picking up non-verbal cues in body language.

Many times you will work with people that have a similar background with regards to their generation. By being aware of the strengths and weaknesses that the immigrants and natives have, you can tailor the way you lead the team. It can be both more beneficial and more challenging when you have a team that crosses generations. This is sometimes called the "digital divide." The breadth of experience and the different styles can ultimately lead to a more balanced and better outcome, but the path there may be more challenging. As with any situation where you have a diverse team, you will need to draw on your skills and abilities to flex your leadership to meet the demands of the team and the project.

In the Work Place

Using the MBTI in the work place can help with team building and it can help the team understand each other better. For optimum results, you can have someone trained in the instrument administer and interpret the results. However, you can also find free assessments online that you can have team members fill out electronically or on paper. Sharing their type in a team meeting is a good way to get to know people, and it builds trust among team members by helping them find common ground while promoting openness and transparency.

If the whole team understands the concepts in the MBTI, it will help them move through challenging situations or conflicts more easily, because they will be able to identify the behaviors associated with the various personality types.

Tools You Can Use

The following web sites have information and on line tests for the Myers-Briggs Type Indicator:

www.humanmetrics.com
www.Keirsey.com

For more information, I recommend *Please Understand Me II: Temperament, Character, Intelligence,* by David Keirsey.

Reflection Exercise

1. Take some time to think about the different types of power you have and how you can best use it to lead your team. You can use the table below to help organize your thoughts.

Type of Power	How it is demonstrated	How I can optimize my power
Formal		
Expert		
Reward/Penalty		
Referent		

2. Think about a time when there was a difference of opinion on your team. Reflect on how the information you learned about personality types, gender differences and the "digital divide" contributed to the difference of opinion. Think about how you can use your understanding of age, gender and personality differences to build a bridge of understanding for the team members so that the differences are constructive for the team.